GERMAN ESSAYS I

AUFKLÄRUNG

WIELAND

LESSING

KANT

GERMAN ESSAYS I

AUFKLÄRUNG

WIELAND

LESSING

KANT

Selected, Edited, and Annotated by

MAX DUFNER
The University of Michigan

VALENTINE C. HUBBS
The University of Michigan

THE MACMILLAN COMPANY, NEW YORK

COLLIER-MACMILLAN LIMITED, LONDON

First Printing

Library of Congress catalog card number: 63-15262

The Macmillan Company, New York
Collier-Macmillan Canada, Ltd., Toronto, Ontario

Printed in the United States of America

DESIGNED BY RONALD FARBER

PREFACE

TODAY, when more and more undergraduates are again reading the "Great Books," it seems appropriate to put into their hands in their foreign language classes reading matter offering an intellectual challenge commensurate with the remainder of their studies. Unfortunately, and partly as a result of the two world wars, it often appears as though many of our students have, at best, the impression that the contribution of German-speaking Europe to the intellectual life of which we are the heirs has been minimal—at worst, they have never heard of any at all. This text is the first of a series whose purpose it is to make easily available in the original German some of those expository writings from the last two centuries considered by many well-read Central Europeans a basic part of Western culture.

As desirable as it may be to read with our advanced classes some of the great classics of German literature, hardly anyone would assert that the students ought to become familiar with belles-lettres only. And while assuredly many of the more elementary "cultural readers" in vogue today mention such names as Kant, Novalis, Alexander von Humboldt, Nietzsche, Jung, and others, these men remain hardly more than names to most students who do not go on to a graduate program in the field of German literature.

The texts in this series are intended as supplements to the work done in third-year classes in college German. At some institutions fourth-semester students will be ready for such material. In any case, no vocabulary has been provided, for if the student is ready to read these rather difficult essays, he will be armed with a good dictionary. However, passages of some syntactical complexity, archaic words, and words of low frequency appear translated in footnotes. The editors have avoided interpretive commentary in the notes except where it appeared necessary for comprehension, since that is the prerogative of the teacher, or better yet, a result of discussion in the classroom under the guidance of the teacher.

In each essay the orthography of the definitive text on which it is based has been retained with no normalization of any kind. The student will soon be accustomed to the peculiarities and begin to enjoy the "flavor" of the author's style.

The essays in this volume are based on the following editions:

Immanuel Kants Werke, edited by Ernst Cassirer. Berlin, 1912 ff., IV.

Lessings Werke, edited by Julius Petersen, W. Olhausen, et al. Berlin, Leipzig, Wien, Stuttgart, 1925, V.

Wieland's Werke, Hempel Edition. Berlin, n.d., XXXII.

CONTENTS

INTRODUCTION

THE German essays in this volume give rather lofty expression to ideals of that intellectual orientation in Germany quite generally identified with the term *Aufklärung*. Like many of their contemporaries, the authors of these pieces, believing that they lived in a new age with great promise for mankind, looked optimistically into a future in which human beings would live full lives in freedom and justice. In one way or another all three essays are concerned with Truth, which was thought to be the master key to such a future. The dark and tortuous paths which had to be traversed by all who would seek it out needed to be illuminated by the use of reason, logic, clear and distinct concepts, acute observation, and often scepticism. Hence the term *Aufklärung*.

In its narrower, more parochial sense, *Aufklärung*

lasted in Germany hardly longer than the century extending roughly from 1680 to 1780. Actually, it was part of a vast European phenomenon, that conscious, self-liberation from dogma, superstition, and ignorance, with its beginnings in the Renaissance and its strongest and most lasting cultivation in France ("l'éclaircissement") and in Britain ("the Enlightenment"). In its broader aspects this movement is still very much alive today, especially in science and politics. It gave birth to new sciences such as chemistry, geology, and meteorology, to the systematization and disciplined cultivation of the life sciences, and to vast achievements in mathematics. Both the theory and practice of parliamentary democracy were worked out by some of its greatest minds, and the American, French, and Russian revolutions were the culmination of some of its most powerful ideas. Perhaps the Enlightenment had an even more important and startling impact on world history, namely that gigantic upheaval which is still proceeding at an ever-accelerating pace—the Industrial Revolution.

It is imperative that we keep in mind this larger historical perspective even though we are concerned here with *Aufklärung* in the stricter sense, that is to say, with its most productive and dynamic phase in eighteenth-century Germany. It is equally important to remember that there were other intellectual positions in that era. Some were opposed to the Enlightenment either entirely or in part (e.g., mysticism and pietism); and others (e.g., sentimentalism and *Sturm und Drang*), while products of *Aufklärung,* were at the same time reactions to it and developed concurrently. This consideration will serve to prevent such confusions as necessarily arise when the student is told in any number of presentations that, with the advent of *Sturm und Drang* in the early seventies, *Aufklärung* was superseded, had become old-fashioned, and its literary representatives, Christoph Martin Wieland, for example, had turned into old fogies. To what extent this is a distortion of history is indicated by some facts. The essay by Kant reprinted in this volume and offering the most noteworthy definition in German of the very spirit of the Enlightenment did not appear until 1784—and that is *an entire decade* after Goethe's novel *Die Leiden des jungen Werthers,* three years after Schiller's *Räuber,* yes, even one year after the latter's composition of *Kabale und Liebe!*

The development of *Aufklärung* reveals especially well the small respect which great ideas have for geographical and linguistic boundaries, for its character was decidedly cosmopolitan. In the seventeenth century the movement found expression in the philosophical systems of the Frenchmen René Descartes (1596–1650) and Nicolas Malebranche (1638–1715), the Englishman Thomas Hobbes (1588–1679), the Dutchman Baruch Spinoza (1632–1677), and the German Gottfried Wilhelm Leibnitz (1646–1716). Whatever system was assumed, the philosopher attempted to make it as consistent as possible, and then, by a process of deduction, to explain reality in accordance with the axioms he considered eternally and universally true. The great thinkers of the eighteenth century, for the most part, replace this *esprit de système* (spirit of the system) with an *esprit systématique* (systematic spirit). Descartes' *Discours de la méthode pour bien conduire sa raison et chercher la vérité dans les sciences* (*Discourse on the Method for Properly Directing the Mind and Seeking Out the Truth in the Sciences*) of

1637 was gradually replaced by Sir Isaac Newton's (1642–1727) *regulae philosophandi* (rules for philosophizing) as the canon supplying the desired method of inquiry. In other words, the methods of the natural sciences were introduced into philosophy. This involves the observation of phenomena in nature, and each phenomenon must be broken down into the constituent parts of which it is the complex.

This new turn in emphasis brought with it a distinct limitation in that the philospoher would henceforth have to forego investigations into the very innermost workings of nature, into the absolute essence of matter ("was die Welt im Innersten zusammenhält," as Goethe expresses it in his *Faust*), or such questions as the nature of the human soul. Philosophical inquiry thus directed its attention less and less to the cosmic and transcendental, and as a result "reason" came to have quite a different meaning from that assigned to it by earlier philosophers.

For Descartes, Spinoza, and Leibnitz, for example, reason was the realm of eternal truths, those truths which the divine being and the human order hold in common. Every instance of the use of reason was an assurance that man has something in common with the transcendental. In the eighteenth century, however, reason is no longer the *possession* of innate ideas which precede experience—a kind of storehouse of the mind; it is considered to be the form of intellectual acquisition; it denotes not the content of knowledge, but rather the *energy* used by the mind to acquire knowledge. This energy, operating through the method of analysis, is the instrument by the use of which man can progress to ever greater heights in knowing the world in which he lives. The predilection in the eighteenth century for writing works of an encyclopedic nature does not altogether contradict this concept of reason; for, besides presenting the public with a large aggregate of knowledge, the writers of such works also provided the factual tools necessary for further inquiry and investigation.

One of the chief concerns of the *Aufklärung* was the validity of perception (*Erkenntnis*) as a philosophical instrument. Descartes tried to define the limits of the human mind; the entire empirical philosophy of Locke grew out of this question, and Kant's *Critique of Pure Reason* represents perhaps the most comprehensive treatment of the problem. The various attempts to provide a rational solution involved an analysis of perception, and thus psychology became fundamental for an understanding of how man acquires knowledge. Because it was necessary to eliminate all religious and metaphysical factors in such investigations, the secularization of philosophy received a mighty impetus.

The Enlightenment is, on the whole, often characterized as being antireligious. To a considerable extent this is certainly true; but although there was a break with traditional forms of faith, many leading thinkers (with the notable exception of the mechanists, e.g., the Frenchman Julien Offray de Lamettrie [1709–1751]) included God—in many instances, to be sure, a deistic God—in their ideas. However, the old dogmatic assertions of the established religions grew more unsatisfactory; and gradually philosophy increased its domain as an independent realm of inquiry. Actually, there developed in the Enlightenment a humanistic attitude toward religion quite similar to that of the Renaissance. Expanded religious toleration resulted from the philosophical effort to discover the true essence of all religion. Thus dogmas came to be thought of as merely the popular, external trappings of faith which hide the concepts that all religions must have as their basis universally. In 1779 Gotthold Ephraim Lessing, author of the second essay in this volume, gave dramatic expression to such views in his play *Nathan der Weise*.

Another phase of the struggle between the enlightened thinkers of the eighteenth century and established theological systems concerned the claim of the latter that they were in *possession* of the truth, an assertion making any strict adherence to their dogmas, so it was thought, worse than sheer ignorance. Furthermore, some of the ideas supported by dogma were shown to be nothing more than superstition. One of the most active spirits in this phase of the Enlightenment was the French writer Pierre Bayle (1647–1706), whose *Historical and Critical Dictionary* of 1695–1697 exerted a vast influence on German minds, both in the original French of later editions and in the German translation published in the years 1741 to 1744 by Johann Christoph Gottsched (1700–1766), the famous professor of poetry, logic, and metaphysics at Leipzig. In the eighteenth century, however, it was Voltaire (1694–1778), probably the most prominent figure of his age, who led this fight and set the pattern for the criticism of religion by the French Encyclopedists, whose leader, Denis Diderot (1713–1784), regarded superstition as more injurious than atheism.

Deism, which divested religion entirely of miracles, mysteries, and secrets, and according to which God exercises no influence in the world or on the beings he has created, became rather popular in England. An eminent adherent in America was Thomas Paine (1737–1809). But in Germany deism failed to gain much influence, since here there remained alive in the sphere of religion those ideas of pre-established harmony that are to be traced to the theory of the monads propounded by Leibnitz, the greatest German philosopher before Kant. Reason and revelation, complementing one another, were both considered to be valid sources of knowledge. German theologians such as Semler, Sack, Spalding, and others did not try to do away with dogma but merely to limit its scope. In Britain the brilliant Scottish historian, philosopher, and political economist David Hume (1711–1776) attacked deism as being based on the concept "human nature," which the deists thought was the same throughout the world. Clearly this was a dogma and so could not stand examination by enlightened philosophical analysis.

An excellent example of a writer who applied the methods of natural science in the field of history is Voltaire, the popularizer on the Continent of Newton's ideas. Particularly Voltaire's *Essai sur les moeurs et l'esprit des nations* (1756) influenced the major historians of his time; and Turgot, Condorcet, Hume, Robertson, and Gibbon were all indebted to him. Until Johann Gottfried Herder (1744–1803) published his *Ideen zur Philosophie der Geschichte der Menschheit* (1784–1791), Voltaire must be considered the foremost and the most original historian. Herder, who read voraciously most of the literature by enlightened authors available to him, based his metaphysics of history on the philosophical notions of Leibnitz, and by combining rational ideas with powerful impulses from mysticism (e.g., from Jakob Boehme [1575–1624]) and pietism, produced a startling intellectual amalgam known as the organic concept of history.

Just as psychology attempted to go back to the very foundations of the human perceptive faculties, and as the new methods of the natural sciences analyzed the phenomena of nature so that they could be studied in their smallest constituent parts, so also political and sociological investigations tried to analyze the problems of the state, its functions, its nature, its relationship to the individual, and the nature and function of ethics. Jean-Jacques Rousseau's *Contrat social* (1762), in its adherence to the notion that man in his primitive state was essentially good, stands opposed to the theories of Hobbes. This English philosopher maintained that the social contract was made through the subjugation of the governed, but Rousseau believed that, if it was to have any value, the social contract must be entered into voluntarily. And within the framework of such a contract the individual can realize the greatest possible amount of freedom and of his potentialities. He believed that freedom was to be achieved only within, and not in opposition to, the law. This regard for the value and dignity of law made Rousseau the real predecessor of Kant, on whom, as is well known, he had very great influence.

It should be noted that Rousseau's thoughts on government proceeded in a manner analogous to that of his contemporaries in other fields. While many of them, for example, sought the essence of religion and found "natural religion," Rousseau, inquiring into the nature of the state, discovered the "state of nature."

The philosophical eighteenth century was also the age of critical analysis of poetry and other forms of literature. In the preceding era Nicolas Boileau-Despréaux (1636–1711) attempted in his work *L'Art poétique* to define poetry scientifically and urged writers to follow the precepts of reason. This critic's intention, however, was most definitely not to assert, as it was later thought to be by second-rate minds, that anyone who "learned the rules" could become a good poet. Boileau wished to bring creative artistic activity within the realm of reason; but unfortunately, especially in Germany, he was often misinterpreted, with the result that this work served more to stifle creative effort than to further it.

Literary criticism aroused so much interest and achieved such prominence in German-speaking Europe that foreigners, surveying the history of German letters, very often receive the impression that German writers were much inclined first to theorize about literary aesthetics and then to compose works to illustrate their theories. The number of such critical works is quite amazing. The more noteworthy include: Gottsched's *Versuch einer Critischen Dichtkunst vor die Deutschen* (1730); Johann Jakob Breitinger's *Critische Dichtkunst* (1740); Johann Jakob Bodmer's *Abhandlung von dem Wunderbaren in der Poesie* (1740); Lessing's *Laokoon oder Über die Grenzen der Mahlerey und Poesie* (1766), and his *Hamburgische Dramaturgie* (1767–1769); and Herder's *Kritische Wälder* (1769). Some of these disquisitions do indeed contain ideas antithetical to the aims of the Enlightenment, but that is not the point here. As is reflected in some of their titles, their critical purpose and method are quite characteristic of the mental bent schooled by *Aufklärung*.

Then too, in this age there came upon the scene in Germany all manner of critical journals and reviews. Among their editors it was especially Wieland who tried, in his *Teutscher Merkur* (1773–1789), not only to inform the public but also to improve its taste in literary matters as well. Here again foreign ventures were taken as models, particularly the important and popular *Mercure de France* (begun in 1672 under the title *Mercure galant*), Pierre Bayle's *Nouvelles de la république des lettres* (1684 ff.), and Addison's and Steele's *Tatler* (1709–1711) and *The Spectator* (1711–1714).

Such then, in kaleidoscopic view, were the more significant intellectual preoccupations of the *Aufklärung*. In such a brief survey the student can only be reminded of concurrent developments in the arts and music. Even though the style in painting, sculpture, architecture, interior decoration, dress, etc., which we call rococo (a refinement of the baroque forms of the previous age), is commonly identified with the period of *Aufklärung*, it is sometimes overlooked that these were also the times that produced the classical music of Franz Josef Haydn (1732–1809) and Wolfgang Amadeus Mozart (1756–1791).

Five years after Kant had answered the question "Was ist Aufklärung?" the citizens of Paris stormed the Bastille. All the social and political reforms urged by the greatest writers of the Enlightenment were now supposedly to be realized. However, the long-awaited millennium did not arrive. In its stead there came the Terror of the French Revolution; and while Reason was enthroned as a goddess, the civilized world stood aghast when news of the terrible excesses came across the borders of France. In Germany the ensuing reaction affected not only political views but the attitudes of even some of the most daring among the literary spirits. All the "enlightened talk" about self-rule, the Rights of Man, and man's innate goodness began to sound hollow and misconceived. Schiller, for example, who two decades earlier had in his drama *Die Räuber* hurled defiance at the law, now wrote in his poem *Das Lied von der Glocke* (1800) some famous lines on revolution, which all through the nineteenth century were mouthed by political reactionaries:

> Gefährlich ist's, den Leu zu wecken,
> Verderblich ist des Tigers Zahn,
> Jedoch der schrecklichste der Schrecken,
> Das ist der Mensch in seinem Wahn.
> Weh denen, die dem Ewigblinden
> Des Lichtes Himmelsfackeln leihn!
> Sie strahlt ihm nicht, sie kann nur zünden
> Und äschert Städt' und Länder ein.

This kind of reaction among the intellectuals, together with the ever greater fascination with the irrational, which had been cultivated throughout the eighteenth century side by side with *Aufklärung* and encouraged by such figures as Hamann, Herder, and Goethe, drew an increasingly large number of thinkers and writers toward an interest in the philosophical idealism created by Kant and developed to its fruition by Fichte, Schelling, and Hegel. Still others were later to succumb to the pessimism of Arthur Schopenhauer. The truly great achievements of *Aufklärung* were relatively forgotten in Germany; and among the romanticists it became fashionable to look back upon that era as an arid, pedantic, and "unpoetic" wasteland. This prejudice was to predominate for over a century in major German writings on the history of literature, philosophy, and culture.

To the student who wishes to pursue the study of *Aufklärung*, the following works are highly recommended:

DE BOOR, H., and R. NEWALD, *Geschichte der deutschen Literatur*. München, 1957, V and VI/1.

The Portable Age of Reason Reader, edited by Crane Brinton. New York, 1956.

CASSIRER, ERNST, *Die Philosophie der Aufklärung.* Tübingen, 1932. This text is also available in English translation by Fritz C. A. Koelln and James P. Pettegrove. Princeton, 1951. Beacon Paperbacks reprinted this translation in 1955.

ERMATINGER, EMIL, *Deutsche Kultur im Zeitalter der Aufklärung.* Potsdam, 1935. In the series: *Handbuch der Kulturgeschichte,* hrsg. von Heinz Kindermann.

HAZARD, PAUL, *The European Mind. The Critical Years 1680–1715,* trans. by J. Lewis May. New Haven, 1952. The original French version appeared in 1935 under the title: *La crise de la conscience européenne.*

SCHÖNBERGER, A., and H. SOEHNER, *The Rococo Age. Art and Civilization of the 18th Century,* trans. from the original German by Daphne Woodward. London, 1960.

WOLFF, HANS M., *Die Weltanschauung der deutschen Aufklärung.* Bern, 1949.

CHRISTOPH MARTIN WIELAND

[1733-1813]

WAS IST WAHRHEIT?

CHRISTOPH MARTIN WIELAND, "one of the noblest and most lucid spirits of the *Aufklärung*" (Ermatinger), was born the son of a pastor in Oberholzheim near Biberach on September 5, 1733. By the time of his death on January 20, 1813 in Weimar, he had at one time been the most celebrated German author, had translated works by Lucian, Horace, and Cicero, and twenty-two of Shakespeare's plays, had edited for many years the popular literary journal *Der teutsche Merkur,* and had enjoyed toward the end of his long life the intimate friendship of the dowager Duchess Ann Amalia.

Wieland's literary production was enormous. Of his nine long novels, the "Bildungsroman" *Geschichte des Agathon* (1766–1794) and the comic *Geschichte der Abderiten* (1773–1781) are important in the history of German literature and still read today. Among his many poetic creations, the verse romance *Oberon* (1780)—translated into English, incidentally, by President John Quincy Adams—is unique, a masterpiece of its kind. After his friend Goethe finished reading the completed poem, he sent it back to Wieland with a laurel wreath.

Perhaps more than any other German writer of his time, Wieland was a humanist; and it is said that only the most distinguished classical philologists surpassed him in his knowledge of the literatures of ancient Greece and Rome. Moreover, the list of authors whose influence has been traced to his own works by literary scholars includes: Chaucer, Shaftesbury, Pope, Fielding, Richardson, Sterne, Bayle, Racine, Voltaire, Rousseau, Cervantes, Ariosto, Tasso, and many others.

Wieland's name is often coupled with that of Lessing, the two being considered the principal German belletristic authors of the *Aufklärung*. But while Lessing's writing, and particularly his expository prose, is generally manfully robust, and cerebral though witty, Wieland's is graceful, light, and humorous, sometimes, however, all too long-winded, and often tentative, some might even say ambivalent, in character. Especially the latter trait made him, even in his own time, appear weak and vacillating when contrasted with Lessing. Actually, his never being quite sure about the truth of a matter, his respect for others' opinions, his synoptic view of the search for truth in the perspective of centuries—these things are precisely what makes Wieland an *Aufklärer* in the very best sense.

The essay *Was ist Wahrheit?* which appeared in the *Teutscher Merkur* of 1778, gives expression to the typical suspicion on the part of the *Aufklärer* of all dogma. The proper attitude of the seeker after truth is modesty, for the genuinely wise know that no one possesses Truth. The more one pursues it, the more surely one becomes convinced it cannot be attained.

Like Lessing, he believed that its pursuit was the most sublime activity of Man.

Bibliography

GRUBER, J. G., *Wielands Leben.* Leipzig, 1815–1816. 2 vols.

SENGLE, F., *Wielands Leben.* Stuttgart, 1949.

VON ABBÉ, DEREK M., *C. M. Wieland.* London, Toronto, Wellington, Sydney, 1961.

WAS IST WAHRHEIT?

DIESE FRAGE ist dadurch, daß sie schon so mannichmal[1] durch den Mund eines Pilatus ging,[2] nichts desto schlechter geworden. Wessen Augen blinzen nicht, wenn er mit dieser Frage überrascht wird? Schon
5 tausend- und zehntausendmal entschieden, wird sie immer wieder als ein *Räthsel* aufgeworfen werden und in zehntausendmal tausend Fällen ein *unauflösbares* bleiben.

Aber so gewiß dies auch ist, wehe Denen, die eine
10 boshafte Freude daran finden, der Schwäche unsers Gesichtes[3] dadurch zu helfen, daß sie uns vollends blind machen! Das Wahrste von Allem, was jemals wahr genannt wurde, ist: daß mitten unter allem Trug von Erscheinungen, Gespenstern und Traumgebilden,
15 wovon wir umgeben sind, jeder Sterbliche gerade so viel Wahrheit auffassen kann, als er zu seiner eignen Nothdurft braucht.

Die Wahrheit ist, wie alles Gute, etwas *Verhältnißmäßiges*. Es kann Vieles für *die menschliche Gattung*
20 wahr sein, was es für höhere oder niedrigere Wesen nicht ist, und ebenso kann etwas von dem einen Menschen mit innigster Ueberzeugung als wahr empfunden und erkannt werden, was ein andrer mit gleich starker Ueberzeugung für Irrthum und Blendwerk
25 hält.

[1] **mannichmal** *oft*

[2] **daß . . . Pilatus ging** *that Pilate's posing of this question has been so often quoted.* (Cf. Bible, John XVIII. 38). This oft-quoted question to which Wieland refers, however, is from Francis Bacon's essay *Of Truth* (1625): "*What is Truth?* said jesting Pilate; and would not stay for an answer."

[3] **Gesicht** *sight*

Die Uebereinstimmung [4] eines Gefühls oder einer Vorstellung mit den allgemein anerkannten Grundwahrheiten der Vernunft ist ebenso wenig als der *Zusammenhang* einer Vorstellung mit allen übrigen, welche die gegenwärtige innere Verfassung eines Menschen ausmachen, ein sicheres Merkmal der Wahrheit.[4] *Jene* [5] läßt uns weiter nichts als die Möglichkeit der Sache erkennen, und *dieser* [6] kann ebensowohl bei der wahresten Vorstellung fehlen, als bei der täuschendsten zugegen sein. Geschiehet nicht öfters, was Jedermann für unmöglich hielt? Und wie oft betrügt die höchste Wahrscheinlichkeit? Erweitert sich nicht der Kreis der Möglichkeiten mit unserer Kenntniß der Natur und mit dem Anwachs unsrer Erfahrungen? Daher zum Theil, daß Leichtgläubigkeit eine charakteristische Eigenschaft des hohen Alters ist, und, was seltsam scheinen mag, neben dem Unglauben besteht, der es nicht weniger ist. *Kinder* sind leichtgläubig aus Unwissenheit dessen, was möglich oder unmöglich ist; *Alte* sind es, weil sie so oft unglaubliche Dinge sich haben zutragen sehen, daß ihnen nichts mehr unglaublich scheint. Jene glauben Alles, weil sie das Mißtrauen noch nicht kennen; bei diesen ist Mißtrauen eine der bittern Früchte des Lebens und macht sie eben so geneigt, an Allem zu zweifeln, als die Erfahrenheit auf der andern Seite, Alles für möglich zu halten.

Die subtilste und kaltblütigste Vernunft hat von jeher die subtilsten Zweifler hervorgebracht. Kar-

[4] **Die Uebereinstimmung . . . Wahrheit** *The agreement of a feeling or a concept with the generally recognized basic truths of reason is no more a certain sign of truth than the connection of a concept with all the others which constitute the present inner frame of mind of a human being.*

[5] **Jene** refers to "*Uebereinstimmung eines Gefühls*" etc.

[6] **dieser** refers to "*der Zusammenhang einer Vorstellung*"

neades, Pyrrho, Sextus, le Vayer, Bayle, Hume [7] waren Männer von großer Vernunft—und ich frage einen Jeden, der sich nicht erst seit ehegestern [8] in der Welt umgesehen hat, was ist es, als gerade die kaltblütige,
5 spitzfindinge,[9] immer zurückhaltende, immer argwöhnische,[10] immer voraussehende, immer raisonnirende Vernunft, was von jeher am Geschäftigsten gewesen ist, *Glauben* und *Liebe*, die einzigen Stützen unsers armen Erdelebens, zu untergraben und umzustürzen?
10 —Wer wollte darum verkennen, wie viel der Mensch diesem Strahle der Gottheit, dem wir den so sehr gemißbrauchten Namen *Vernunft* geben, schuldig ist? Allerdings kann sie nichts dafür, daß Sophisten und Witzlinge [11] von jeher ihren natürlichen Gebrauch in
15 den unnatürlichen verwandelt haben; aber da der Mensch nun einmal diesen unglücklichen Hang hat, wehe ihm, wenn seine *Vernunft* die *einzige* Führerin seines Lebens ist!

Man hat sich schon so lange über die Leute aufge-
20 halten, die ein unerklärbares *inneres* Licht zum Leitstern ihres Glaubens und Lebens machen; man hat sie in Schimpf und Ernste bestritten, zu Boden gespottet

[7] **Karneades** (213–129 B.C.), philosopher from Cyrene in Africa; a Stoic philosopher who later became at Platonist. He was particularly interested in truth in such matters as transcended man's reasoning powers; **Pyrrho** (c. 365–275 B.C.), Greek philosopher from Elis, founder of the sceptical school of philosophy; **Sextus** (c. 200–250 A.D.), Roman philosopher and Sceptic; **François de la Mothe le Vayer** (1588–1672), a French sceptic; **Pierre Bayle** (1647–1706), author of the famous *Dictionnaire historique et critique,* which exerted great influence in eighteenth-century Germany; **David Hume** (1711–1776), English philosopher, political economist and historian. He is best known for his *History of England* and *An Inquiry Concerning Human Understanding.*

[8] **vorgestern.**

[9] *cavilling*

[10] *distrustful*

[11] **Witzlinge** *wiseacres*

und zu Boden raisonnirt: und dennoch haben unleugbar alle Menschen etwas, das die Stelle eines solchen innern Lichts vertritt, und das ist—*das innige Bewußtsein dessen, was wir fühlen.* Unter allen Kennzeichen der Wahrheit ist dies unleugbar das *sicherste;* 5 vorausgesetzt, daß ein Mensch überhaupt gesund und des Unterschieds seiner Empfindungen und Einbildungen sich bewußt ist. Beweiset einem Menschen, seine Vernunft sei eine Zauberin, die ihn alle Augenblicke täusche und irre führe—das wird ihn noch nicht 10 verwirren; beweiset ihm, daß er seinen Sinnen, seinem innern Gefühle nicht trauen dürfe—das verwirrt ihn! Und wenn es möglich wäre, daß Euer Beweis seine volle Wirkung auf diesen Menschen thäte, so bliebe nichts übrig, als ihn stehendes Fußes [12] ins Tollhaus zu 15 führen.

Zum Glück ist der Glaube an sein eignes Gefühl gerade das, was sich der Mensch am Schwersten und Seltensten nehmen läßt, ja, was sich schwerlich irgend ein Mensch, wie schwach er immer sei, in irgend einem 20 Falle nehmen läßt, wo er sich *innigst bewußt ist,* daß er gefühlt hat. Das Einzige, wodurch er dahin gebracht werden könnte, an der Wahrheit seines eignen Gefühls oder, was ebendasselbe ist, *an sich selbst* und *seinem eignen Dasein* zu zweifeln, wäre der Fall, in welchen 25 (in einer der arabischen Erzählungen, die Herr Galland [13] *le Dormeur éveillé* betitelt) der Khalife Harun Alraschid den armen Kaufmann Abu-Hassan durch einen Betrug, den Dieser unmöglich entdecken konnte, versetzte, der aber auch, unvermeidlicherweise, die 30 Folge hatte, daß Abu-Hassan darüber in *Raserei* verfiel

[12] **stehendes Fußes** *right away*
[13] **Antoine Galland** (1646–1715), a French Orientalist and archeologist. He was the first European translator of the *Arabian Nights.*

und nicht anders als durch Entdeckung des Betrugs wieder hergestellt werden konnte.

Aber, sagt man, wie häufig sind die Fälle, wo ein Mensch durch seine Sinne oder durch sein *inneres* 5 *Gefühl* betrogen wird? wo er, ohne darum ganz wahnsinnig zu sein, für *Empfindung* hält, was bloße *Einbildung* ist? wo er einen Gegenstand in dem verfälschenden Lichte der Leidenschaft oder des Vorurtheils sieht? u. s. w.

10 Unstreitig sind diese Fälle häufig. Und eben so haüfig geschieht es, daß von *Zweien*, die einander durch ihr *Gefühl* widerlegen, Beide betrogen werden; daß, während der Eine Jupiter ist und die sündige Welt mit Feuer zu zerstören droht—der Andre uns dagegen 15 seines gnädigen Schutzes versichert, weil er Neptunus ist, der durch seine Gewässer den Brand gar leicht wieder löschen kann. —Aber alle diese Fälle vermögen gleichwol nichts gegen die Grundfeste des allgemeinen Menschensinnes; und der Glaube, den ein Jeder an sein 20 eignes Gefühl hat, bleibt nichts desto minder in seiner vollen Kraft. Ich kann von *der Natur*, von unsichtbaren *Mächten*, kurz, von *Ursachen, die ich nicht kenne*, getäuschet werden; aber so lange ich mir bewußt bin, daß ich etwas gefühlt, beschaut, betastet habe— 25 so *glaube ich meinem Gefühl* mehr als einer ganzen Welt, die dagegen zeugte, und als allen Philosophen, die mir *a priori* [14] beweisen wollten, ich träume oder rase.

Freilich ist es *verdächtig*, wenn ein Mensch *in Sachen* 30 *des Gefühls* eine ganze Welt oder, was nicht viel besser ist, die *vernünftigsten* Leute in der Welt wider sich hat, oder wenn er in sehr zusammengesetzten und verwickelten Dingen, in Sachen, die von scharfer Zer-

[14] a priori by logical means alone as distinct from proof based on experience (or experiment).

gliederung und von richtiger Zusammenstellung und Verknüpfung einer Menge von Begriffen abhangen, welche selbst wieder Resultate von einer Menge andrer sind, —es ist, sage ich, verdächtig, wenn Jemand in Sachen *dieser Art* dem Wege der *scharfen Untersuchung* ausweicht und immer nur auf *sein Gefühl* oder *unser Gefühl* provocirt.[15] Aber was wollen wir mit ihm anfangen, wenn er uns nicht zur Untersuchung *stehen* will? Und wenn wir ihn auch dazu nöthigen könnten, wer soll zwischen *seiner Empfindung* und der *unsrigen* oder zwischen *unsrer Vernunft* und seinem *Gefühl* oder *Glauben* Richter sein? Wo ist der *Areopagus,*[16] wo sind die *Amphiktyonen,*[17] deren Ausspruch man in solchen Fällen sich unterwerfen *könnte, wollte, müßte?*

In metaphysischen und ästhetischen Dingen, das ist in Sachen, wo das Meiste auf Einbildung und Sinnesart ankommt, wäre das Billigste, einen Jeden im Besitz und Genuß dessen, was er für Wahrheit hält, ruhig und ungekränkt zu lassen, solange er Andre in Ruhe läßt. Wer hat ein Recht in seines Nachbars Verzäunung[18] einzudringen und den Frieden seiner Hausgötter[19] zu

[15] **Freilich . . . provocrit** *To be sure it is suspicious if a person in emotional matters has against him a whole world or, what is not much better, the most reasonable people in the world, or if in very complex and involved things, in matters which depend upon sharp analysis and correct synthesis and concatenation of a number of concepts which in themselves are in turn the results of a number of others—it is, I say, suspicious, if someone in matters of this kind avoids the avenue of clear investigation and continues to appeal only to his feeling or to ours.*

[16] **Areopagus** the oldest and most famous court in ancient Athens.

[17] **Amphiktyonen** members of an association of communities for the protection of a common religious center in ancient Greece, for example, Delphi. Here the word is used, more or less, in the sense of adjudicators.

[18] **Verzäunung** *enclosure*

[19] **Hausgötter** called the *Lares Familiares* by the Romans. They were the guardian spirits of the household. By **Hausgötter** Wieland means here simply a person's private notions.

stören? Mag doch seine *Melusine* [20] einen Fischschwanz unter ihrem Rocke tragen, was geht das Andre an? Aber freilich, sobald der Mann ins Kreuz und in die Quere [21] auf allen Landstraßen herumreitet und Alle, die da
5 ruhig ihres Weges gehen, anhalten und mit eingelegter Lanze zwingen will, zu bekennen, daß *seine* Prinzessin schöner ist als die ihrige, oder wol gar, daß sie allein schön, und jedes andre Gesicht ein Meerkatzengesicht ist, —das ist etwas sehr Unangenehmes für Leute, die
10 keine Lust haben, sich zu balgen: [22] und wiewol die irrenden Ritter, die solche Thaten thun, in den Augen kluger Leute ihre Entschuldigung unter dem Hute tragen; so mögen sie sich's doch selbst zuschreiben, wenn sie dann und wann unter Mauleseltreiber und
15 Preller [23] fallen, die nicht so säuberlich mit ihnen verfahren.

Die Wahrheit (wenn wir noch einen Augenblick mit dem Gleichniß spielen dürfen) flieht vor der keichenden [24] Verfolgung ihrer feurigsten Liebhaber, um in die
20 Arme Dessen zu laufen, der sie weder erwartete, noch suchte. Der einfältigste Menschensinn findet sie am Ersten und genießt ihrer, wie der Luft, die er athmet, ohne daran zu denken. Der Grübler, der sie überall sucht, findet sie nirgends, just darum, weil er sich nicht
25 einbilden kann, daß sie ihm so nahe sei. Und sobald ihrer zwei sich über ihren ausschließenden Besitz in die Haare gerathen, so darf man sicher rechnen, daß

[20] **Melusine** heroine of a medieval tale in Jean d'Arras' *Chronique de la princesse* (1387). At regular intervals she was changed from the hips downward into the form of a serpent, a fact which her husband was not to know. Wieland' s word ***Fischschwanz*** is somewhat typical of his humor.

[21] **ins Kreuz und in die Quere** *helter-skelter*

[22] **sich zu balgen = sich zu streiten**

[23] **Preller** *cheaters, swindlers*

[24] **keichenden = keuchenden**

sie es ihnen macht, wie Angelika den beiden Rittern im Ariost:[25] während die tapfern Männer sich bei den Köpfen haben, geht die Dame davon und lacht über Beide.

Ist dies Bild zu komisch? —Nun, so ist hier ein andres, das ebenso gut zur Sache paßt. Die *Wahrheit* ist weder hier, noch da,—sie ist, wie die Gottheit und das Licht, worin sie wohnt, *allenthalben: ihr Tempel ist die Natur,* und wer nur *fühlen* und seine Gefühle zu *Gedanken* erhöhen und seine Gedanken in *ein Ganzes zusammenfassen* und *ertönen* lassen kann, ist ihr *Priester,* ihr *Zeuge,* ihr *Organ.* Keinem offenbart sie sich *ganz;* Jeder sieht sie nur stückweise, nur von *hinten* oder nur den *Saum ihres Gewandes*—aus einem andern Punkt, in einem andern Lichte; Jeder vernimmt nur *einige* Laute ihres Göttermundes, Keiner die nämlichen—[26]

Und was haben wir also zu thun?

Anstatt mit einander zu hadern, wo die *Wahrheit* sei, *wer* sie besitze? *wer* sie in ihrem schönsten Lichte gesehen? die meisten und deutlichsten Laute von ihr vernommen habe, —lasset uns in Frieden zusammen gehen oder, wenn wir des Gehens genug haben, unter den nächsten Baum uns hinsetzen und einander offenherzig und unbefangen erzählen, was Jeder von ihr gesehen und gehört hat oder gesehen zu haben glaubt, und ja nicht böse darüber werden, wenn sich's von ungefähr entdeckt, daß wir falsch gesehen oder gehört oder gar (wie es brünstigen Liebhabern, die ihr zu nahe kommen wollen, öfters begegnet) *eine Wolke für die Göttin* umarmt haben.

[25] **Ariost** (1474–1533), Lodovico Ariosto, a great Italian poet. The incident referred to here takes place in Canto I of his famous poem *Orlando Furioso.*

[26] **die nämlichen** *the same ones*

Vor Allem aber, lieben [sic] Brüder, hüten wir uns vor der Thorheit, unsere *Meinungen* für Axiome und *unumstößliche Wahrheiten* anzusehen und Andern als solche vorzutragen. Es ist ein widerlicher, harter Ton
5 um den *Ton der Unfehlbarkeit:* [27] aber es giebt einen, der noch unausstehlicher ist—der Ton eines *Energumenen,*[28] der, auf dem heiligen Dreifuße [29] sitzend, alle seine Reden als Göttersprüche von sich giebt. *Bescheidenheit* würde uns vor dem einen und vor dem
10 andern sicher stellen.

Wenn ein Mann auch so alt wäre wie Nestor,[30] und so weise wie siebenmal sieben Weise zusammengenommen, so müßt' er doch—eben darum, weil er so alt und so weise wäre—einsehen gelernt haben: daß man
15 immer weniger von den Dingen *begreift,* je mehr man davon *weiß;* daß gegen *eine lichte Stelle,* die wir *in der unermeßlichen Nacht der Natur* erblicken, zehntausend in *Dämmerung* und zehnmal zehntausend im *Dunkeln* vor uns liegen, und daß wenn wir uns auch von diesem
20 Erdklümpchen, das uns ein ungeheures Weltall scheint, bis zur Sonne aufschwingen und in ihrem Lichte dies ganze Planetensystem mit allem seinem Inhalt und Zubehör so deutlich übersehen könnten, wie Jemand von der Spitze einer Terrasse seinen Garten übersieht,
25 dies nämliche *Planetensystem* nun abermal nichts mehr für uns wäre als—*eine lichte Stelle in der unermeßlichen Nacht der Natur.*

Und wenn dann der weise Mann in einer so langen Lehrzeit auch noch gelernt hätte, daß eben diese

[27] **den Ton der Unfehlbarkeit** Construe this as the subject.

[28] **Energumenen** a person possessed of spirits who speak through him, a religious fanatic.

[29] **Dreifuß** *a tripod,* part of the paraphernalia of the ancient Greek oracle, e.g., at Delphi.

[30] **Nestor** In Homer's *Iliad* the eldest of all the Greek warriors before the walls of Troy. He was greatly respected because of his wisdom in councils of war.

Unermeßlichkeit und *Unbegreiflichkeit,* die für uns Erdebewohner eine Eigenschaft der ganzen Natur ist, sich auch in jedem *einzelnen Stäubchen* befindet; daß in jedem einzelnen Punkte der Natur Strahlen aus allen übrigen zusammenlaufen, und wie unbegreiflich 5 alle diese Strahlen, Beziehungen, Aus- und Einflüsse aller Dinge auf jedes und jeden Dinges auf alle einander durchschneiden und durchkreuzen; wie unmöglich es also ist, nur eine einzige Erscheinung, eine einzige Bewegung oder Wirkung eines einzigen Theil- 10 chens der Natur recht zu erkennen, ohne zugleich die ganze Natur ebenso zu durchschauen, wie Der, in dem sie lebt und webt und ist: beim Himmel! ich denke, das müßte den weisen Mann *bescheiden* gemacht haben, und es sollte mich nicht wundern, wenn er alle 15 seine Urtheile und Meinungen in einem Tone vorbrächte, den ein Mann wie Elihu, der Sohn Barachiel von Bus, des Geschlechts Ram,[31] mit allem Unwillen eines erhlichen überzeugten Dogmatikers für baren Skepticismus halten müßte. 20

Ein Anderes ist, wenn ein Esel, dem der Herr den Mund aufthut,[32] mit Zuversichtlichkeit spricht; dafür ist aller Respect zu tragen; denn es ist nicht der Esel, sondern ein Gott (dem es gleich viel gelten kann, durch welches Organ er sich hörbar macht), der durch den 25 Esel spricht. Einem Menschen aber—es sei denn, er könne uns beweisen, daß er sich im Falle des besagten Esels befinde—ziemt es, ungeachtet[33] des aufgerichteten Angesichts und des Blicks gen Himmel, der ihm gegeben ist, von Zeit zu Zeit auf seine Füße zu sehen 30 und—bescheiden zu sein.

[31] **Elihu** Cf. Bible, Job XXXIIff.

[32] **dem . . . aufthut** *whom God speaks through.* Cf. Bible, Numbers XXII:28ff.

[33] **ungeachtet** *in spite of*

GOTTHOLD EPHRAIM LESSING

[1729-1781]

DIE ERZIEHUNG DES MENSCHENGESCHLECHTS

GOTTHOLD EPHRAIM LESSING was born on the twenty-second of January, 1729, at Kamenz in Saxony. He attended the *Fürstenschule* of St. Afra in Meissen where he distinguished himself as a brilliant student. In the autumn of 1746 he went to the University of Leipzig and commenced the study of theology. While a student at Leipzig, Lessing became interested in the theater. His friendship with actors resulted in his having to flee from Leipzig to escape being put into debtor's prison for having stood surety for loans which the actors never repaid. But this experience also gave him an opportunity to try his hand at writing drama and to learn much about the requirements of good theater. After a short stay at the University of Wittenberg, Lessing went to Berlin. In 1748 he began his long career as a journalist and free-lance writer in this great city.

Lessing was one of the greatest men in the history

of German letters and a true product of the Enlightenment. In his search for truth he was incessant, indefatigable, and inexorable. He believed that the quest for truth was ennobling. It mattered little whether the goal were ever reached; indeed, Lessing did not believe that it would ever be reached. He once wrote:

> Wenn Gott in seiner Rechten alle Wahrheit und in seiner Linken den einzigen immer regen Trieb nach Wahrheit, obschon mit dem Zusatze, mich immer und ewig zu irren, verschlossen hielte und spräche zu mir: „Wähle!" ich fiele ihm mit Demut in seine Linke und sagte: „Vater, gib! die reine Wahrheit ist ja doch nur für dich allein!"

Lessing was not only an astute critic, but also a brilliant scholar, poet, aesthetician, philosopher, and theologian. As a critic he is internationally known and recognized. His essay on the proper provinces of poetry and painting, *Laokoon oder Über die Grenzen der Mahlerey und Poesie* (1766), cleared up much of the confusion of the time concerning the boundaries of the arts and presented the field of aesthetics with a new principle which undoubtedly influenced its later development. Lessing also helped to develop a new direction in German literature that became independent of French Classicism by espousing the freer style of English literature. In the theater Lessing introduced the *bürgerliches Trauerspiel* with his drama *Miss Sara Sampson* (1755). With his *Minna von Barnhelm* (1767) he presented Germany with one of its masterpieces of comedy.

Lessing's scholarship enriched many fields. His liberal views and defense of deism, his vindications of many a maligned or forgotten scholar, his predilection for publishing the truth regardless of the consequences to himself made him an enemy of many an empty pedant and frequently added to the uncertainty of his already precarious material existence.

Many of Lessing's most brilliant works in the field of religious philosophy owe their existence to a controversy with Pastor Goeze of St. Catherine's Church in Hamburg. The controversy was precipitated by some fragments from an unpublished work of the late deist, Professor Samuel Reimarus. Lessing published these fragments in 1777 without revealing the author's name, and he was immediately attacked as their author. The bitter controversy which followed was finally halted by a ducal order, but not before Lessing had proved that the orthodox pastor was no match for him. In order to circumvent censorship, Lessing turned once again to the theater. In his noble drama of religious tolerance, *Nathan der Weise* (1779), he presented his final arguments.

Die Erziehung des Menschengeschlechts, published in 1780, is a later embodiment of Lessing's religious philosophy and a monument to the most characteristic ideals of the Enlightenment in Germany: the concept of progress and the use of human reason even in the realm of religion. In its day Lessing's essay was eagerly devoured by many of the rationalistic deists, who had finally found a champion of the type of liberal Christianity they espoused. But not all minds of that period looked with favor upon Lessing's liberal concepts. The theologians of the Enlightenment were attempting to reconcile orthodoxy with the empiricism of the scientific method. Lessing felt that these two spheres were diametrically opposed and thus completely incompatible. He therefore sought to discover religious truth by ignoring the irrational dogma of orthodoxy and applying the faculty of reason to the problem of religion.

Bibliography

FITTBOGEN, G., *Die Religion Lessings*. Leipzig, 1923.

LEISEGANG, H., *Lessings Weltanschauung*. Leipzig, 1931.

SIME, J., *G. E. Lessing: His Life and Writings*. London, 1877. 2 vols.

DIE ERZIEHUNG DES MENSCHENGESCHLECHTS

1

Was die Erziehung bei dem einzeln Menschen ist, ist die Offenbarung [1] bei dem ganzen Menschengeschlechte.

2

Erziehung ist Offenbarung, die dem einzeln Menschen geschieht: und Offenbarung ist Erziehung, die dem Menschengeschlechte geschehen ist, und noch geschieht.

3

Ob die Erziehung aus diesem Gesichtspunkte zu betrachten, in der Pädagogik Nutzen haben kann, will ich hier nicht untersuchen. Aber in der Theologie kann es gewiß sehr großen Nutzen haben und viele Schwierigkeiten heben,[2] wenn man sich die Offenbarung als eine Erziehung des Menschengeschlechts vorstellet.

[1] *revelation*
[2] **heben** *lift, remove, eliminate*

4

Erziehung gibt dem Menschen nichts, was er nicht auch aus sich selbst haben könnte: [3] sie gibt ihm das, was er aus sich selber haben könnte, nur geschwinder und leichter. Also gibt auch die Offenbarung dem Menschengeschlechte nichts, worauf die menschliche Vernunft, sich selbst überlassen,[4] nicht auch kommen würde: sondern sie gab und gibt ihm die wichtigsten dieser Dinge nur früher. 5

5

Und so wie es der Erziehung nicht gleichgültig ist,[5] in welcher Ordnung sie die Kräfte des Menschen entwickelt; wie sie dem Menschen nicht alles auf einmal beibringen kann: ebenso hat auch Gott bei seiner Offenbarung eine gewisse Ordnung, ein gewisses Maß halten müssen.[6] 10

6

Wenn auch [7] der erste Mensch mit einem Begriffe von einem Einigen Gotte sofort ausgestattet wurde: so konnte doch dieser mitgeteilte, und nicht erworbene 15

[3] **was er nicht auch aus sich selbst haben könnte** *that he could not also generate out of his own being*

[4] **sich selbst überlassen** *left to itself*

[5] **so wie es . . . ist** *just as it is not a matter of indifference to education*

[6] **ebenso . . . halten müssen** *also God likewise has had to keep a certain order in his revelation, has had to keep within certain limits.*

[7] **Wenn auch** *Even if*

Begriff [8] unmöglich lange in seiner Lauterkeit [9] bestehen. Sobald ihn [10] die sich selbst überlassene menschliche Vernunft zu bearbeiten anfing, zerlegte sie den Einzigen Unermeßlichen in mehrere Ermeß-
5 lichere,[11] und gab jedem dieser Teile ein Merkzeichen.[12]

7

So entstand natürlicherweise Vielgötterei und Abgötterei.[13] Und wer weiß, wie viele Millionen Jahre sich die menschliche Vernunft noch in diesen Irrwegen würde herumgetrieben haben; ohngeachtet [14] überall und zu
10 allen Zeiten einzelne Menschen erkannten, daß es Irrwege waren: wenn es Gott nicht gefallen hätte, ihr durch einen neuen Stoß eine bessere Richtung zu geben.[15]

8

Da er aber einem jeden einzeln Menschen sich nicht
15 mehr offenbaren konnte, noch wollte: So wählte er sich ein *einzelnes Volk* zu seiner besonderen Erziehung;

[8] **dieser mitgeteilte . . . Begriff** *this imparted concept which was not acquired* (i.e., was not a product of reason)
[9] *purity, clearness*
[10] **ihn = den Begriff**
[11] **zerlegte . . . Ermeßlichere** *it reduced the single infinite one to several, more finite ones*
[12] *sign, stamp*
[13] **Vielgötterei und Abgötterei** *polytheism and idolatry*
[14] **ohngeachtet = ungeachtet,** *in spite of the fact that*
[15] Construe: **Und wer weiß, wie viele Millionen Jahre sich die menschliche Vernunft noch in diesen Irrwegen würde herumgetrieben haben, . . . wenn es Gott nicht gefallen hätte, ihr [der Vernunft] durch einen neuen Stoß, usw.**

und eben das ungeschliffenste, das verwildertste,[16] um mit ihm ganz von vorne anfangen zu können.

9

Dies war das israelitische Volk, von welchem man gar nicht einmal weiß, was es für einen Gottesdienst in Ägypten hatte. Denn an dem Gottesdienste der Ägyptier durften so verachtete Sklaven nicht teilnehmen: und der Gott seiner Väter war ihm gänzlich unbekannt geworden.

10

Vielleicht, daß ihm die Ägyptier allen Gott,[17] alle Götter ausdrücklich untersagt hatten; es in den Glauben gestürzt hatten, es habe gar keinen Gott, gar keine Götter; Gott, Götter haben, sei nur ein Vorrecht der bessern Ägyptier: und das, um es mit so viel größerm Anscheine[18] von Billigkeit[19] tyrannisieren zu dürfen. —Machen Christen es mit ihren Sklaven noch itzt[20] viel anders?—

11

Diesem rohen Volke also ließ sich Gott anfangs bloß als den Gott seiner Väter ankündigen, um es nur erst

[16] **und eben das ungeschliffenste, das verwildertste [Volk]; ungeschliffen** *crude;* **verwildert** *uncultivated*
[17] **allen Gott** *any god*
[18] *appearance*
[19] *justice, right*
[20] **itzt = jetzt**

mit der Idee eines auch ihm zustehenden Gottes [21] bekannt und vertraut [22] zu machen.

12

Durch die Wunder, mit welchen er es aus Ägypten führte, und in Kanaan einsetzte, bezeugte er sich ihm [23] 5 gleich darauf als einen Gott, der mächtiger sei, als irgend ein andrer Gott.

13

Und indem er fortfuhr, sich ihm als den Mächtigsten von allen zu bezeugen, —welches doch nur *einer* sein kann, —gewöhnte er es allmählich [24] zu dem Begriffe 10 des *Einigen.*

14

Aber wie weit war dieser Begriff des Einigen noch unter dem wahren transzendentalen Begriffe des Einigen, welchen die Vernunft so spät erst aus dem Begriffe des Unendlichen mit Sicherheit schließen 15 lernen! [25]

[21] **eines auch ihm zustehenden Gottes** *of a God also belonging to them*
[22] *familiar*
[23] **ihm = dem Volk**
[24] *gradually*
[25] **[hat] schließen lernen** *learned to deduce*

15

Zu dem wahren Begriffe des Einigen—wenn sich ihm auch schon die Bessern des Volks mehr oder weniger näherten—konnte sich doch das Volk lange nicht erheben: und dieses war die einzige wahre Ursache,[26] warum es so oft seinen Einigen Gott verließ, 5 und den Einigen, d. i. Mächtigsten, in irgend einem andern Gotte eines andern Volks zu finden glaubte.

16

Ein Volk aber, das so roh, so ungeschickt zu abgezognen [27] Gedanken war, noch so völlig in seiner Kindheit war, was war es für einer *moralischen* Erziehung 10 fähig? [28] Keiner andern,[29] als die [30] dem Alter der Kindheit entspricht. Der Erziehung [31] durch unmittelbare [32] sinnliche [33] Strafen und Belohnungen.

17

Auch hier also treffen Erziehung und Offenbarung zusammen. Noch konnte Gott seinem Volke keine 15 andere Religion, kein anders Gesetz geben, als eines,

[26] *cause*
[27] *abstract*
[28] **was war es für einer . . . fähig?** *of what kind of moral education was it (i.e.,* **das Volk***) capable?*
[29] Genitive because like **einer moralischen Erziehung** it is dependent upon **fähig.**
[30] **diejenige, die**
[31] Also dependent upon **fähig.**
[32] *immediate*
[33] *material, tangible, addressed to the senses*

durch dessen Beobachtung oder Nichtbeobachtung es
hier auf Erden glücklich oder unglücklich zu werden
hoffte oder fürchtete. Denn weiter als auf dieses Leben
gingen noch seine Blicke nicht. Es wußte von keiner
5 Unsterblichkeit [34] der Seele; es sehnte sich [35] nach
keinem künftigen Leben. Ihm aber nun schon diese
Dinge zu offenbaren, welchen seine Vernunft noch so
wenig gewachsen war: [36] was würde es bei Gott anders
gewesen sein, als der Fehler des eiteln Pädagogen, der
10 sein Kind lieber übereilen und mit ihm prahlen,[37] als
gründlich [38] unterrichten will.

18

Allein wozu, wird man fragen, diese Erziehung eines
so rohen Volkes, eines Volkes, mit welchem Gott so
ganz von vorne anfangen mußte? Ich antworte: um in
15 der Folge der Zeit einzelne Glieder [39] desselben so viel
sicherer zu Erziehern aller übrigen Völker brauchen zu
können. Er erzog in ihm die künftigen Erzieher des
Menschengeschlechts. Das wurden Juden, das konnten
nur Juden werden, nur Männer aus einem so erzogenen
20 Volke.

19

Denn weiter.[40] Als das Kind unter Schlägen und

[34] *immortality*
[35] **sich sehnen nach** *to long for*
[36] **welchen . . . gewachsen war** *for which their reason was still hardly a match.*
[37] *boast, show off*
[38] *thoroughly*
[39] *generations, members*
[40] *Let us continue*

Liebkosungen aufgewachsen und nun zu Jahren des Verstandes gekommen war, stieß es der Vater auf einmal in die Fremde; und hier erkannte es auf einmal das Gute, das es in seines Vaters Hause gehabt und nicht erkannt hatte. 5

20

Während daß Gott sein erwähltes Volk durch alle Staffeln[41] einer kindischen Erziehung führte: waren die andern Völker des Erdbodens bei dem Lichte der Vernunft ihren Weg fortgegangen. Die meisten derselben waren weit hinter dem erwählten Volke zurückgeblieben: nur einige waren ihm zuvorgekommen. Und auch das geschieht bei Kindern, die man für sich[42] aufwachsen läßt; viele bleiben ganz roh; einige bilden sich zum Erstaunen selbst.[43] 10

21

Wie aber[44] diese glücklichern Einige nichts gegen den Nutzen und die Notwendigkeit der Erziehung beweisen: so beweisen die wenigen heidnischen Völker, die selbst in der Erkenntnis Gottes vor dem erwählten Volke noch bis itzt einen Vorsprung[45] zu haben schienen, nichts gegen die Offenbarung. Das Kind der Erziehung fängt mit langsamen aber sichern Schritten an; es holt manches glücklicher[46] organisierte Kind 15 20

[41] *stages*
[42] **für sich** *by themselves*
[43] **einige . . . selbst** *some educate themselves to an astonishing degree.*
[44] *But just as*
[45] **einen Vorsprung haben vor** *to be ahead of*
[46] *more advantageously*

der Natur spät ein; aber es holt es doch ein, und ist alsdann nie wieder von ihm einzuholen.[47]

22

Auf gleiche Weise.[48] Daß,[49]—die Lehre von der Einheit Gottes beiseite gesetzt, welche in den Büchern des
5 Alten Testaments sich findet, und sich nicht findet—daß,[49] sage ich, wenigstens die Lehre von der Unsterblichkeit der Seele, und die damit verbundene Lehre von Strafe und Belohnung in einem künftigen Leben, darin völlig fremd sind: beweiset ebensowenig wider
10 den göttlichen Ursprung dieser Bücher. Es kann demohngeachtet[50] mit allen darin enthaltenen Wundern und Prophezeiungen seine gute Richtigkeit haben.[51] Denn laßt uns setzen,[52] jene Lehren würden nicht allein darin *vermißt*, jene Lehren wären auch
15 sogar *nicht* einmal *wahr;* laßt uns setzen, es wäre wirklich für die Menschen in diesem Leben alles aus: wäre darum das Dasein Gottes minder erwiesen? stünde es darum Gotte minder frei, würde es darum Gotte minder ziemen,[53] sich der zeitlichen Schicksale irgend
20 eines Volks aus diesem vergänglichen Geschlechte unmittelbar anzunehmen? Die Wunder, die er für die Juden tat, die Prophezeiungen, die er durch sie aufzeichnen ließ, waren ja nicht bloß für die wenigen sterblichen Juden, zu deren Zeiten sie geschahen und
25 aufgezeichnet wurden: er hatte seine Absichten damit

[47] **ist einzuholen** *can be overtaken*
[48] **Auf gleiche Weise** *by the same token, similarly*
[49] *the fact that*
[50] *nevertheless*
[51] **kann seine gute Richtigkeit haben** *may well be correct*
[52] **laßt uns setzen** *let us suppose*
[53] **würde es . . . ziemen** *would it therefore be less fitting for God*

auf das ganze jüdische Volk,[54] auf das ganze Menschengeschlecht, die hier auf Erden vielleicht ewig dauern sollen, wenn schon jeder einzelne Jude, jeder einzelne Mensch auf immer dahinstirbt.

23

Noch einmal. Der Mangel jener Lehren in den Schriften des Alten Testaments beweiset wider ihre Göttlichkeit nichts. Moses war doch von Gott gesandt, obschon die Sanktion seines Gesetzes sich nur auf dieses Leben erstreckte. Denn warum weiter? [55] Er war ja nur an das *israelitische* Volk, an das *damalige* israelitische Volk gesandt: und sein Auftrag war den Kenntnissen, den Fähigkeiten, den Neigungen dieses *damaligen* israelitischen Volks, sowie der Bestimmung des *künftigen,* vollkommen angemessen.[56] Das ist genug.

24

So weit hätte *Warburton* [57] auch nur gehen müssen, und nicht weiter. Aber der gelehrte Mann überspannte den Bogen.[58] Nicht zufrieden, daß der Mangel jener Lehren der göttlichen Sendung Mosis nichts schade: er sollte ihm die göttliche Sendung Mosis sogar be-

[54] **er hatte . . . Volk** *he was aiming therewith at the entire Jewish people*

[55] *For why should it extend any further?*

[56] **war angemessen** *was proportionate to, was adapted to*

[57] **William Warburton** (1698–1779), English prelate and friend of Alexander Pope. He became Bishop of Gloucester in 1759. Lessing is referring to his *Divine Legation of Moses.*

[58] **den Bogen überspannen** *to go too far, overdo something*

weisen. Und wenn er diesen Beweis noch aus der Schicklichkeit eines solchen Gesetzes für ein solches Volk zu führen gesucht hätte![59] Aber er nahm seine Zuflucht[60] zu einem von Mose bis auf Christum ununterbrochen fortdaurenden Wunder,[61] nach welchem Gott einen jeden einzeln Juden gerade so glücklich oder unglücklich gemacht habe, als es dessen Gehorsam oder Ungehorsam gegen das Gesetz verdiente. Dieses Wunder habe den Mangel jener Lehren, ohne welche kein Staat bestehen könne, ersetzt; und eine solche Ersetzung eben beweise, was jener Mangel, auf den ersten Anblick, zu verneinen scheine.

25

Wie gut war es, daß *Warburton* dieses anhaltende Wunder, in welches er das Wesentliche der israelitischen Theokratie setzte, durch nichts erhärten,[62] durch nichts wahrscheinlich machen konnte. Denn hätte er das gekonnt; wahrlich—alsdann erst hätte er die Schwierigkeit unauflöslich gemacht. —Mir Wenigstens. —Denn was die Göttlichkeit der Sendung Mosis wiederherstellen sollte, würde an der Sache selbst zweifelhaft gemacht haben, die Gott zwar damals nicht mitteilen, aber doch gewiß auch nicht erschweren wollte.[63]

[59] **Und wenn . . . hätte** [How much better it would have been] *if he had sought to derive his proof from the suitability of such a law for such a people!*

[60] **Zuflucht nehmen** *to take refuge*

[61] **zu . . . Wunder** *in a miracle continuing without interruption from Moses to Christianity*

[62] *prove*

[63] **würde an der Sache . . . wollte** *would have cast doubt upon the very thing which, to be sure, God did not yet want to impart, but certainly also did not want to make more difficult.*

26

Ich erkläre mich an dem Gegenbilde der Offenbarung.[64] Ein Elementarbuch für Kinder darf gar wohl dieses oder jenes wichtige Stück der Wissenschaft oder Kunst, die es vorträgt, mit Stillschweigen übergehen, von dem der Pädagog urteilte, daß es den Fähigkeiten 5
der Kinder, für die er schrieb, noch nicht angemessen[65] sei. Aber es darf schlechterdings nichts enthalten, was den Kindern den Weg zu den zurückbehaltnen wichtigen Stücken versperre oder verlege.[66] Vielmehr müssen ihnen alle Zugänge zu denselben sorgfältig offen 10
gelassen werden:[67] und sie nur von einem einzigen dieser Zugänge ableiten, oder verursachen, daß sie denselben[68] später betreten, würde allein die Unvollständigkeit des Elementarbuchs zu einem wesentlichen Fehler desselben machen. 15

27

Also auch konnten in den Schriften des Alten Testaments, in diesen Elementarbüchern für das rohe und im Denken ungeübte israelitische Volk, die Lehre[n] von der Unsterblichkeit der Seele und künftigen Vergeltung gar wohl mangeln: aber enthalten durften sie 20
schlechterdings nichts, was das Volk, für das sie ge-

[64] **Ich erkläre . . . Offenbarung** *I explain my point of view by the counterpart of revelation.*

[65] *suited*

[66] **versperren oder verlegen würde**

[67] **Vielmehr . . . gelassen werden** *On the contrary, every access to them must be carefully left open for them*

[68] **denselben = den Weg zu den zurückbehaltenen wichtigen Stücken**

schrieben waren, auf dem Wege zu dieser großen Wahrheit auch nur verspätet hätte. Und was hätte es, wenig zu sagen,[69] mehr dahin *verspätet,* als wenn jene wunderbare Vergeltung in diesem Leben darin wäre
5 versprochen, und von dem wäre versprochen worden, der nichts verspricht, was er nicht hält? [70]

28

Denn wenn schon aus der ungleichen Austeilung der Güter dieses Lebens, bei der auf Tugend und Laster [71] so wenig Rücksicht [72] genommen zu sein scheinet, eben
10 nicht der strengste Beweis für die Unsterblichkeit der Seele und für ein anders Leben, in welchem jener Knoten sich auflöse, zu führen: [73] so ist doch wohl gewiß, daß der menschliche Verstand ohne jenen Knoten noch lange nicht—und vielleicht auch nie—auf
15 bessere und strengere Beweise gekommen wäre. Denn was sollte ihn antreiben können, diese bessern Beweise zu suchen? Die bloße Neugierde? [74]

29

Der und jener Israelite mochte freilich wohl die göttlichen Versprechungen und Androhungen,[75] die

[69] **wenig zu sagen** *to say the least*
[70] **und von dem . . . hält** *and had been promised by the one who makes no promises that he does not keep?*
[71] **Tugend und Laster** *virtue and vice*
[72] *consideration*
[73] **zu führen [ist]**
[74] *curiosity*
[75] *threats*

sich auf den gesamten Staat bezogen,[76] auf jedes einzelne Glied desselben erstrecken, und in dem festen Glauben stehen, daß wer fromm sei auch glücklich sein müsse, und wer unglücklich sei, oder werde, die Strafe seiner Missetat trage, welche sich sofort wieder in Se- 5 gen verkehre, sobald er von seiner Missetat ablasse. —Ein solcher [77] scheinet den Hiob [78] geschrieben zu haben; denn der Plan desselben ist ganz in diesem Geiste.—

30

Aber unmöglich durfte die tägliche Erfahrung diesen 10 Glauben bestärken: oder es war auf immer bei dem Volke, das diese Erfahrung hatte, auf *immer* um die Erkennung und Aufnahme der ihm noch ungeläufigen Wahrheit geschehen.[79] Denn wenn der Fromme schlechterdings glücklich war, und es zu seinem Glücke 15 doch wohl auch mit gehörte, daß seine Zufriedenheit keine schrecklichen Gedanken des Todes unterbrachen, daß er alt und *lebenssatt* [80] starb: wie konnte er sich nach einem andern Leben sehnen? wie konnte er über etwas nachdenken, wornach er sich nicht sehnte? 20 Wenn aber der Fromme darüber nicht nachdachte: wer sollte es denn? Der Bösewicht? der die Strafe seiner Missetat fühlte und, wenn er dieses Leben ver-

[76] **die sich auf den gesamten Staat bezogen** *which referred to the entire state*

[77] **Ein solcher Israelite**

[78] Book of Job

[79] **oder . . . geschehen** *or among the people having this experience the recognition and acceptance of the truth which was still unfamiliar to them was doomed forever.*

[80] *tired of life, "full of days."* Cf. Genesis xxxv.29.

wünschte, so gern auf jedes andere Leben Verzicht tat? [81]

31

Weit weniger verschlug es,[82] daß der und jener Israelite die Unsterblichkeit der Seele und künftige 5 Vergeltung, weil sich das Gesetz nicht darauf bezog, geradezu und ausdrücklich leugnete. Das Leugnen eines Einzeln—wäre es auch ein Salomo [83] gewesen, —hielt den Fortgang des gemeinen Verstandes nicht auf, und war an und für sich selbst schon ein Beweis, 10 daß das Volk nun einen großen Schritt der Wahrheit näher gekommen war. Denn Einzelne leugnen nur, was Mehrere in Überlegung ziehen; und in Überlegung ziehen, warum [84] man sich vorher ganz und gar nicht bekümmerte, ist der halbe Weg zur Erkenntnis.

32

15 Laßt uns auch bekennen, daß es ein heroischer Gehorsam ist, die Gesetze Gottes beobachten, bloß weil es Gottes Gesetze sind, und nicht, weil er die Beobachter derselben hier und dort zu belohnen verheißen [85] hat; sie beobachten,[86] ob man schon an der künftigen Be-

[81] **so gern . . . tat** *so gladly renounced every other life*
[82] **Weit . . . es** *It mattered far less*
[83] **Salomo** *Solomon*
[84] **warum** = **worum**
[85] **verheißen** *promised*
[86] Both **die Gesetze Gottes beobachten** and **sie beobachten** depend upon **daß es ein heroischer Gehorsam ist.** *It is an heroic obedience to observe them if one has already completely despaired of a future reward and is not quite so certain of a temporal one.*

lohnung ganz verzweifelt, und der zeitlichen auch nicht so ganz gewiß ist.

33

Ein Volk, in diesem heroischen Gehorsame gegen Gott erzogen, sollte es nicht bestimmt,[87] sollte es nicht vor allen andern fähig sein, ganz besondere göttliche Absichten auszuführen?—Laßt den Soldaten, der seinem Führer blinden Gehorsam leistet, nun auch von der Klugheit seines Führers überzeugt werden, und sagt, was dieser Führer mit ihm auszuführen sich nicht unterstehen [88] darf?—

34

Noch hatte das jüdische Volk in seinem Jehova mehr den Mächtigsten, als den Weisesten aller Götter verehrt; noch hatte es ihn als einen eifrigen [89] Gott mehr gefürchtet, als geliebt: auch dieses zum Beweise, daß die Begriffe, die es von seinem höchsten einigen Gott hatte, nicht eben die rechten Begriffe waren, die wir von Gott haben müssen. Doch nun war die Zeit da, daß diese seine Begriffe erweitert, veredelt, berichtiget werden sollten, wozu sich Gott eines ganz natürlichen Mittels bediente; eines bessern richtigern Maßstabes, nach welchem es ihn zu schätzen Gelegenheit bekam.[90]

[87] **bestimmt sein** *be destined*
[88] **sich unterstehen** *to dare*
[89] *zealous*
[90] **wozu . . . bekam** *for which purpose God employed a completely natural means, a better, more proper criterion by which they had an opportunity to assess him.*

35

Anstatt daß es ihn bisher nur gegen die armseligen Götzen der kleinen benachbarten rohen Völkerschaften geschätzt [91] hatte, mit welchen es in beständiger Eifersucht lebte: fing es in der Gefangenschaft unter dem
5 weisen Perser [92] an, ihn gegen das Wesen aller Wesen [93] zu messen, wie das eine geübtere Vernunft erkannte und verehrte.[94]

36

Die Offenbarung hatte seine Vernunft geleitet, und nun erhellte die Vernunft auf einmal seine Offen-
10 barung.

37

Das war der erste wechselseitige Dienst, den beide einander leisteten; und dem Urheber beider ist ein solcher gegenseitiger Einfluß so wenig unanständig, daß ohne ihn eines von beiden überflüssig sein würde.[95]

[91] **schätzen gegen etwas** *to compare*

[92] **Cyrus the Great** (died 529 B.C.) In 539 B.C. Cyrus captured Babylon and eventually freed the Jews who had been brought there in captivity by Nebuchadnezzar in 588.

[93] **das Wesen aller Wesen** *the supreme being.* The Persians and Chaldeans believed in a superior being as lord of the universe. See note 102.

[94] **wie . . . verehrte** *which a more practiced power of reasoning recognized and venerated.*

[95] **und dem Urheber . . . sein würde** *and to the originator of the two* (i.e., **Vernunft und Offenbarung**) *such a mutual influence is so little out of place that without it one of the two would be superfluous.*

38

Das in die Fremde geschickte Kind sahe andere Kinder, die mehr wußten, die anständiger lebten,[96] und fragte sich beschämt: warum weiß ich das nicht auch? warum lebe ich nicht auch so? Hätte in meines Vaters Hause man mir das nicht auch beibringen; dazu mich nicht auch anhalten[97] sollen? Da sucht es seine Elementarbücher wieder vor, die ihm längst zum Ekel geworden, um die Schuld auf die Elementarbücher zu schieben. Aber siehe! es erkennet, daß die Schuld nicht an den Büchern liege, daß die Schuld ledig[98] sein eigen sei, warum es nicht längst ebendas wisse, ebenso lebe.

39

Da die Juden nunmehr,[99] auf Veranlassung der reinern persischen Lehre,[100] in ihrem Jehova nicht bloß den größten aller Nationalgötter, sondern Gott erkannten; da sie ihn als solchen in ihren wieder hervorgesuchten heiligen Schriften um so eher finden und andern zeigen konnten, als er wirklich darin war; da sie vor allen sinnlichen Vorstellungen desselben einen ebenso großen Abscheu bezeugten, oder doch in diesen Schriften zu haben angewiesen wurden, als die Perser nur immer hatten: was Wunder,[101] daß sie vor den

[96] **die anständiger lebten** *who had a higher standard of living*
[97] **anhalten** *to urge, encourage, to keep a person to a thing*
[98] **ledig = lediglich** *solely*
[99] **nunmehr** *by this time*
[100] **auf Veranlassung . . . Lehre** *motivated by the purer Persian doctrine*
[101] *is it any wonder*

Augen des Cyrus mit einem Gottesdienste Gnade fanden, den er zwar noch weit unter dem reinen Sabäismus,[102] aber doch auch weit über die groben Abgöttereien zu sein erkannte, die sich dafür [103] des verlaßnen
5 Landes der Juden bemächtiget hatten?

40

So erleuchtet über ihre eignen unerkannten Schätze kamen sie zurück, und wurden ein ganz andres Volk, dessen erste Sorge es war, diese Erleuchtung unter sich dauerhaft zu machen. Bald war an Abfall [104] und
10 Abgötterei unter ihm [105] nicht mehr zu denken. Denn man kann einem Nationalgott wohl untreu werden, aber nie Gott, sobald man ihn einmal erkannt hat.

41

Die Gottesgelehrten haben diese gänzliche Veränderung des jüdischen Volks verschiedentlich [106] zu
15 erklären gesucht; und einer,[107] der die Unzulänglichkeit aller dieser verschiednen Erklärungen sehr wohl gezeigt hat, wollte endlich "die augenscheinliche Erfül-

[102] *Sabianism.* A form of religion which was once widespread in ancient Persia and Chaldea. It taught of the oneness of God as thought behind the universe. In actual practice the religion was, however, polytheistic because the people worshipped the heavenly bodies.
[103] *in its place*
[104] *backsliding*
[105] *among them* (i.e., **dem Volk**)
[106] *variously, in different ways*
[107] **und einer . . . angeben** *and one, who very ably showed the inadequacy of all these different explanations, finally wanted to assign the evident fulfillment of the oral and written prophecies of the Babylonian captivity and deliverance therefrom as the true cause of it* (*i.e., of the change*).

lung der über die Babylonische Gefangenschaft und die Wiederherstellung aus derselben ausgesprochnen und aufgeschriebnen Weissagungen" für die wahre Ursache derselben angeben.[107] Aber auch diese Ursache kann nur insofern die wahre sein, als sie die nun erst veredelten Begriffe von Gott voraussetzt. Die Juden mußten nun erst erkannt haben, daß Wundertun und das Künftige vorhersagen,[108] nur Gott zukomme; [109] welches beides sie sonst auch den falschen Götzen [110] beigelegt hatten, wodurch [111] eben Wunder und Weissagungen bisher [112] nur einen so schwachen, vergänglichen Eindruck auf sie gemacht hatten.

42

Ohne Zweifel waren die Juden unter den Chaldäern und Persern auch mit der Lehre von der Unsterblichkeit der Seele bekannter geworden. Vertrauter mit ihr wurden sie in den Schulen der griechischen Philosophen in Ägypten.

43

Doch da es mit dieser Lehre, in Ansehung ihrer heiligen Schriften, die Bewandtnis nicht hatte, die es mit der Lehre von der Einheit und den Eigenschaften Gottes gehabt hatte; da jene von dem sinnlichen Volke darin war gröblich übersehen worden, diese aber ge-

[108] **das Künftige vorhersagen** *predicting the future*
[109] **nur Gott zukomme** *was only within God's province*
[110] *idols*
[111] *as a result of which*
[112] *up to now*

sucht sein wollte; da auf diese noch *Vorübungen* nötig gewesen waren, und also nur *Anspielungen* und *Fingerzeige* stattgehabt hatten: so konnte der Glaube an die Unsterblichkeit der Seele natürlicherweise nie der
5 Glaube des gesamten Volks werden.[113] Er war und blieb nur der Glaube einer gewissen Sekte desselben.

44

Eine *Vorübung* auf die Lehre von der Unsterblichkeit der Seele nenne ich z. E.[114] die göttliche Androhung, die Missetat des Vaters an seinen Kindern bis ins dritte
10 und vierte Glied zu strafen. Dies gewöhnte die Väter in Gedanken mit ihren spätesten Nachkommen[115] zu leben, und das Unglück, welches sie über diese Unschuldige gebracht hatten, vorauszufühlen.

45

Eine *Anspielung* nenne ich, was bloß die Neugierde
15 reizen und eine Frage veranlassen sollte. Als die oft vorkommende Redensart, *zu seinen Vätern versammlet werden,* für sterben.

[113] **Doch da es . . . des gesamten Volks werden** *But since, with respect to their holy scriptures, the case with this doctrine was not the same as it had been with the doctrine of the unity and attributes of God, since the former doctrine had been grossly overlooked in the scriptures by these sentient people and since the latter doctrine required being sought after—and inasmuch as advance preparation had been necessary for this but only allusions and hints had occurred in the scriptures—belief in the immortality of the soul could not naturally become the belief of all the people.*

[114] **zum Exempel** *for example*

[115] *posterity*

46

Einen *Fingerzeig* nenne ich, was schon irgend einen Keim enthält, aus welchem sich die noch zurückgehaltne Wahrheit entwickeln läßt. Dergleichen war Christi Schluß aus der Benennung *Gott Abrahams, Isaaks* und *Jakobs*.[116] Dieser Fingerzeig scheint mir 5 allerdings in einen strengen Beweis ausgebildet werden zu können.

47

In solchen Vorübungen, Anspielungen, Fingerzeigen besteht die *positive* Vollkommenheit eines Elementarbuchs; so wie die oben erwähnte Eigenschaft, daß es 10 den Weg zu den noch zurückgehaltenen Wahrheiten nicht erschwere, oder versperre, die *negative* Vollkommenheit desselben war.

48

Setzt hierzu noch die Einkleidung[117] und den Stil —1) die Einkleidung der nicht wohl zu übergehenden 15 abstrakten Wahrheiten[118] in Allegorien und lehrreiche einzelne Fälle, die als wirklich geschehen erzählet werden. Dergleichen sind die Schöpfung,[119] unter dem

[116] **Dergleichen . . . Jakobs** *Such was the deduction of Christ from the designation* God of Abraham, Isaac and Jacob.

[117] *wording*

[118] **der . . . Wahrheiten** *of the abstract truths that cannot very well be overlooked*

[119] *creation*

Bilde des werdenden Tages; die Quelle des moralischen Bösen, in der Erzählung vom verbotnen Baume; der Ursprung der mancherlei Sprachen, in der Geschichte vom Turmbaue zu Babel, usw.

49

5 2) den Stil —bald plan[120] und einfältig, bald poetisch, durchaus voll Tautologien, aber solchen, die den Scharfsinn üben, indem sie bald etwas anders zu sagen scheinen, und doch das nämliche sagen, bald das nämliche zu sagen scheinen, und im Grunde etwas 10 anders bedeuten oder bedeuten können: —

50

Und ihr habt alle gute Eigenschaften eines Elementarbuchs sowohl für Kinder, als für ein kindisches Volk.

51

Aber jedes Elementarbuch ist nur für ein gewisses 15 Alter. Das ihm entwachsene Kind länger, als die Meinung gewesen,[121] dabei zu verweilen,[122] ist schädlich. Denn um dieses auf eine nur einigermaßen nützliche Art tun zu können, muß man mehr hineinlegen, als darin liegt; mehr hineintragen, als es fassen kann.

[120] *plain*
[121] **als die Meinung gewesen** [war] *than had been intended*
[122] **verweilen** *to make stay, to keep*

Man muß der Anspielungen und Fingerzeige zu viel suchen und machen,[123] die Allegorien zu genau ausschütteln, die Beispiele zu umständlich deuten,[124] die Worte zu stark pressen. Das gibt dem Kinde einen kleinlichen, schiefen, spitzfindigen[125] Verstand; das 5 macht es geheimnisreich, abergläubisch, voll Verachtung gegen alles Faßliche[126] und Leichte.

52

Die nämliche Weise, wie die Rabbinen ihre heiligen Bücher behandelten! Der nämliche Charakter, den sie dem Geiste ihres Volks dadurch erteilten! 10

53

Ein beßrer Pädagog muß kommen, und dem Kinde das erschöpfte Elementarbuch aus den Händen reißen. —Christus kam.

54

Der Teil des Menschengeschlechts, den Gott in *einen* Erziehungsplan hatte fassen wollen —er hatte aber nur 15 denjenigen in einen fassen wollen, der durch Sprache, durch Handlung, durch Regierung, durch andere natürliche und politische Verhältnisse in sich bereits ver-

[123] **Man muß . . . machen** *One must search out and make too many allusions and hints*
[124] **zu umständlich deuten** *expound too minutely*
[125] **kleinlich** *pedantic;* **schief** *distorted;* **spitzfindig** *hypercritical*
[126] *everything tangible, everything comprehensible*

bunden war—war zu dem zweiten großen Schritte der Erziehung reif.

55

Das ist: dieser Teil des Menschengeschlechts war in der Ausübung seiner Vernunft so weit gekommen, daß
5 er zu seinen moralischen Handlungen edlere, würdigere Bewegungsgründe bedurfte und brauchen konnte, als zeitliche Belohnung und Strafen waren, die ihn bisher geleitet hatten. Das Kind wird Knabe. Leckerei und Spielwerk weicht der aufkeimenden Begierde, ebenso
10 frei, ebenso geehrt, ebenso glücklich zu werden, als es sein älteres Geschwister [127] sieht.

56

Schon längst waren die Bessern von jenem *Teile* des Menschengeschlechts gewohnt, sich durch einen *Schatten* solcher edlern Bewegungsgründe regieren zu
15 lassen. Um nach diesem Leben auch nur in dem Andenken seiner Mitbürger fortzuleben, tat der Grieche und Römer alles.

57

Es war Zeit, daß ein andres *wahres* nach diesem Leben zu gewärtigendes Leben [128] Einfluß auf seine
20 Handlungen gewönne.

[127] Lessing is referring specifically to the Persians and generally to any people who were more advanced than the Hebrews.
[128] **ein andres . . . Leben** *another true life to be expected after this life*

58

Und so ward Christus der erste *zuverlässige,*[129] *praktische Lehrer* der Unsterblichkeit der Seele.

59

Der erste *zuverlässige* Lehrer. —Zuverlässig durch die Weissagungen, die in ihm erfüllt schienen; zuverlässig durch die Wunder, die er verrichtete; zuverlässig 5 durch seine eigene Wiederbelebung[130] nach einem Tode, durch den er seine Lehre versiegelt hatte. Ob wir noch itzt diese Wiederbelebung, diese Wunder beweisen können: das lasse ich dahingestellt sein.[131] So, wie ich es dahingestellt sein lasse, wer die Person dieses 10 Christus gewesen. Alles das kann damals zur *Annehmung* seiner Lehre wichtig gewesen sein: itzt ist es zur Erkennung der Wahrheit dieser Lehre so wichtig nicht mehr.

60

Der erste praktische Lehrer. —Denn ein anders ist, 15 die Unsterblichkeit der Seele, als eine philosophische Spekulation, vermuten, wünschen, glauben: ein anders, seine innern und äußern Handlungen darnach einrichten.

[129] *reliable*
[130] *resurrection*
[131] **das lasse . . . sein** *I shall not go any further into that, I put that aside.*

61

Und dieses wenigstens lehrte Christus zuerst. Denn ob es gleich bei manchen Völkern auch schon vor ihm eingeführter Glaube war, daß böse Handlungen noch in jenem Leben bestraft würden: so waren es doch
5 nur solche, die der bürgerlichen Gesellschaft Nachteil brachten, und daher auch schon in der bürgerlichen Gesellschaft ihre Strafe hatten. Eine innere Reinigkeit des Herzens in Hinsicht auf ein andres Leben zu empfehlen, war ihm allein vorbehalten.

62

10 Seine Jünger haben diese Lehre getreulich fortgepflanzt. Und wenn sie auch kein ander Verdienst hätten, als daß sie einer Wahrheit, die Christus nur allein für die Juden bestimmt zu haben schien, einen allgemeinern Umlauf unter mehrern Völkern verschafft
15 hätten: so wären sie schon darum unter die Pfleger und Wohltäter des Menschengeschlechts zu rechnen.

63

Daß sie aber diese eine große Lehre noch mit andern Lehren versetzten, deren Wahrheit weniger einleuchtend, deren Nutzen weniger erheblich war: wie konnte
20 das anders sein? Laßt uns sie darum nicht schelten, sondern vielmehr mit Ernst untersuchen: ob nicht selbst diese beigemischten Lehren ein neuer *Richtungsstoß* für die menschliche Vernunft geworden [waren].

64

Wenigstens ist es schon aus der Erfahrung klar, daß die neutestamentlichen Schriften, in welchen sich diese Lehren nach einiger Zeit aufbewahret fanden, das zweite beßre Elementarbuch für das Menschengeschlecht abgegeben haben, und noch abgeben. 5

65

Sie haben seit siebzehnhundert Jahren den menschlichen Verstand mehr als alle andere Bücher beschäftiget; mehr als alle andere Bücher erleuchtet, sollte es auch nur durch das Licht sein,[132] welches der menschliche Verstand selbst hineintrug. 10

66

Unmöglich hätte irgend ein ander Buch unter so verschiednen Völkern so allgemein bekannt werden können: und unstreitig hat das, daß so ganz ungleiche Denkungsarten [133] sich mit diesem nämlichen Buche beschäftigten, den menschlichen Verstand mehr fortgeholfen, als wenn jedes Volk für sich besonders [134] sein eignes Elementarbuch gehabt hätte. 15

67

Auch war es höchst nötig, daß jedes Volk dieses

[132] **sollte es . . . sein** *even if it should only be by means of the light*
[133] **Denkungsarten = Denkarten** *mentalities*
[134] **für sich besonders** *for themselves in particular*

Buch eine Zeitlang für das *Non plus ultra* seiner Erkenntnisse halten mußte. Denn dafür muß auch der Knabe sein Elementarbuch vors erste ansehen;[135] damit die Ungeduld, nur fertig zu werden, ihn nicht
5 zu Dingen fortreißt, zu welchen er noch keinen Grund gelegt hat.

68

Und was noch itzt höchst wichtig ist: —Hüte dich, du fähigeres Individuum, der du an dem letzten Blatte dieses Elementarbuches stampfest und glühest,[136] hüte
10 dich, es deine schwächere[n] Mitschüler merken zu lassen,[137] was du witterst, oder schon zu sehn beginnest.

69

Bis sie dir nach sind,[138] diese schwächere[n] Mitschüler; —kehre lieber noch einmal selbst in dieses
15 Elementarbuch zurück, und untersuche, ob das, was du nur für Wendungen[139] der Methode, für Lückenbüßer[140] der Didaktik hältst, auch wohl nicht etwas Mehrers ist.

[135] **Denn dafür . . . ansehen** *For the schoolboy too must regard his primer as such at first.* **vors erste** = **fürs erste**

[136] **stampfen** *to paw the ground* (*as a horse*), *i.e., to be impatient, to charge ahead like a fiery steed;* **glühen** *to be ardent.*

[137] **hüte dich . . . lassen** *be careful not to let your weaker fellow students notice.*

[138] **Bis . . . sind** *Until such a time as they have achieved your degree of insight.* (Literally: "until they are up to you.")

[139] *phrasing, phraseology*

[140] *stopgaps*

70

Du hast in der Kindheit des Menschengeschlechts an der Lehre von der Einheit Gottes gesehen, daß Gott auch bloße Vernunftswahrheiten [141] unmittelbar offenbaret; oder verstattet [142] und einleitet, daß bloße Vernunftswahrheiten als unmittelbar geoffenbarte 5 Wahrheiten eine Zeitlang gelehret werden: um sie geschwinder zu verbreiten, und sie fester zu gründen.

71

Du erfährst, in dem Knabenalter des Menschengeschlechts, an der Lehre von der Unsterblichkeit der Seele, das nämliche. Sie wird in dem zweiten bessern 10 Elementarbuche als Offenbarung *geprediget*, nicht als Resultat menschlicher Schlüsse *gelehret*.[143]

72

So wie wir zur Lehre von der Einheit Gottes nunmehr des Alten Testaments entbehren können; so wie wir allmählich zur Lehre von der Unsterblichkeit der Seele 15 auch des Neuen Testaments entbehren zu können anfangen: könnten in diesem nicht noch mehr dergleichen Wahrheiten vorgespiegelt werden, die wir als Offenbarungen so lange anstaunen sollen, bis sie die

[141] *truths which can be derived rationally*
[142] **verstatten** *to allow, permit*
[143] **nicht als . . . gelehret** *not taught as the end result of human deductions.*

Vernunft aus ihren andern ausgemachten Wahrheiten herleiten und mit ihnen [hat] verbinden lernen? [144]

73

Z. E. die Lehre von der Dreieinigkeit.[145] —Wie, wenn [146] diese Lehre den menschlichen Verstand, nach
5 unendlichen Verirrungen rechts und links, nur endlich auf den Weg bringen sollte, zu erkennen, daß Gott in dem Verstande,[147] in welchem endliche Dinge *eins* sind, unmöglich *eins* sein könne; daß auch seine Einheit eine transzendentale Einheit sein müsse, welche eine
10 Art von Mehrheit nicht ausschließt? —Muß Gott wenigstens nicht die vollständigste Vorstellung von sich selbst haben? d. i. eine Vorstellung, in der sich alles befindet, was in ihm selbst ist? Würde sich aber alles in ihr finden, was in ihm selbst ist, wenn auch von
15 seiner *notwendigen Wirklichkeit,* sowie von seinen übrigen Eigenschaften, sich bloß eine Vorstellung, sich bloß eine Möglichkeit fände? Diese Möglichkeit erschöpft das Wesen seiner übrigen Eigenschaften: aber auch seiner notwendigen Wirklichkeit? Mich dünkt
20 nicht. —Folglich kann entweder Gott gar keine vollständige Vorstellung von sich selbst haben: oder diese vollständige Vorstellung ist ebenso notwendig wirklich, als er es selbst ist usw. —Freilich ist das Bild von mir im Spiegel nichts als eine leere Vorstellung von mir,
25 weil es nur das von mir hat, wovon Lichtstrahlen auf

[144] **könnten in diesem . . . lernen** *might there still not be more such truths presented in the latter which we are to wonder at as revelations until our rational faculty has learned how to deduce them from its other established truths and to link them up with them?*

[145] **die Lehre von der Dreieinigkeit** *the doctrine of the holy Trinity*

[146] **Wie, wenn** *Suppose*

[147] **in dem Verstande** *in the sense*

seine Fläche fallen. Aber wenn denn nun dieses Bild *alles*, alles ohne Ausnahme hätte, was ich selbst habe: würde es sodann auch noch eine leere Vorstellung, oder nicht vielmehr eine wahre Verdopplung meines Selbst sein? —Wenn ich eine ähnliche Verdopplung in 5 Gott zu erkennen glaube: so irre ich mich vielleicht nicht sowohl, als daß die Sprache meinen Begriffen unterliegt;[148] und so viel bleibt doch immer unwidersprechlich, daß diejenigen, welche die Idee davon populär machen wollen, sich schwerlich faßlicher und 10 schicklicher hätten ausdrücken können,[149] als durch die Benennung eines *Sohnes,* den Gott von Ewigkeit zeugt.

74

Und die Lehre von der Erbsünde.[150] —Wie, wenn uns endlich alles überführte, daß der Mensch auf der *ersten* 15 *und niedrigsten* Stufe seiner Menschheit schlechterdings so Herr seiner Handlungen nicht sei, daß er moralischen Gesetzen folgen könne?

75

Und die Lehre von der Genugtuung[151] des Sohnes. —Wie, wenn[152] uns endlich alles nötigte, anzuneh- 20

[148] **so irre . . . unterliegt** *I am perhaps not so much in error, as that my language is incapable of expressing my concepts adequately*
[149] **sich schwerlich . . . können** *could hardly have expressed themselves more comprehensibly and suitably*
[150] *the doctrine of original sin*
[151] *the doctrine of the atonement*
[152] **Wie, wenn** *What if, Suppose*

men: daß Gott,[153] ungeachtet jener ursprünglichen Unvermögenheit des Menschen, ihm dennoch moralische Gesetze lieber [hat] geben [wollen], und ihm alle Übertretungen in Rücksicht auf seinen *Sohn,* d. i.
5 in Rücksicht auf den selbständigen Umfang aller seiner Vollkommenheiten, gegen den und in dem jede Unvollkommenheit des Einzeln verschwindet, lieber [hat] verzeihen wollen; als daß er sie ihm nicht [hat] geben [wollen], und ihn von aller moralischen Glückseligkeit
10 [hat] ausschließen wollen,[153] die sich ohne moralische Gesetze nicht denken läßt?

76

Man wende nicht ein,[154] daß dergleichen Vernünfteleien über die Geheimnisse der Religion untersagt sind. —Das Wort Geheimnis bedeutete in den ersten Zeiten
15 des Christentums ganz etwas anders, als wir itzt darunter verstehn; und die Ausbildung geoffenbarter Wahrheiten in Vernunftswahrheiten ist schlechterdings notwendig, wenn dem menschlichen Geschlechte damit geholfen sein soll. Als sie geoffenbaret wurden, waren
20 sie freilich noch keine Vernunftswahrheiten; aber sie wurden geoffenbaret, um es zu werden. Sie waren gleichsam das Fazit,[155] welches der Rechenmeister seinen Schülern voraussagt, damit sie sich im Rechnen

[153] **daß Gott . . . ausschließen wollen** *that God, in spite of that original inability of man, nevertheless chose to give him moral laws and to forgive him all transgressions in consideration of his Son, that is, in consideration of the self-dependent totality of all his perfections, compared to which and in which any imperfection of an individual disappears, rather than not to give them to him and to exclude him from all moral bliss.*

[154] **Man . . . ein** *one should not object*

[155] *sum, total*

einigermaßen darnach richten können. Wollten sich die Schüler an dem vorausgesagten Fazit begnügen: so würden sie nie rechnen lernen, und die Absicht, in welcher der gute Meister ihnen bei ihrer Arbeit einen Leitfaden [156] gab, schlecht erfüllen. 5

77

Und warum sollten wir nicht auch durch eine Religion, mit deren historischen Wahrheit, wenn man will, es so mißlich aussieht, gleichwohl auf nähere und bessere Begriffe vom göttlichen Wesen, von unsrer Natur, von unsern Verhältnissen zu Gott, geleitet werden 10 können, auf welche die menschliche Vernunft von selbst nimmermehr gekommen wäre?

78

Es ist nicht wahr, daß Spekulationen über diese Dinge jemals Unheil gestiftet, und der bürgerlichen Gesellschaft nachteilig geworden. —Nicht den Speku- 15 lationen: dem Unsinne, der Tyrannei, diesen Spekulationen zu steuern; Menschen, die ihre eigenen hatten, nicht ihre eigenen zu gönnen, ist dieser Vorwurf zu machen.

79

Vielmehr sind dergleichen Spekulationen—mögen 20 sie im einzeln doch ausfallen, wie sie wollen—un-

[156] *guide*

streitig die *schicklichsten* Übungen des menschlichen Verstandes überhaupt, solange das menschliche Herz überhaupt höchstens nur vermögend ist, die Tugend wegen ihrer ewigen glückseligen Folgen zu lieben.

80

5 Denn bei dieser Eigennützigkeit des menschlichen Herzens, auch den Verstand nur allein an dem üben wollen, was unsere körperlichen Bedürfnisse betrifft,[157] würde ihn mehr stumpfen, als wetzen heißen. Er will schlechterdings an geistigen Gegenständen geübt sein, 10 wenn er zu seiner völligen Aufklärung gelangen, und diejenige Reinigkeit [158] des Herzens hervorbringen soll, die uns, die Tugend um ihrer selbst willen zu lieben, fähig macht.

81

Oder soll das menschliche Geschlecht auf diese 15 höchste[n] Stufen der Aufklärung und Reinigkeit nie kommen? Nie?

82

Nie? —Laß mich diese Lästerung [159] nicht denken, Allgütiger! [160] —Die Erziehung hat ihr *Ziel;* bei dem

[157] **was . . . betrifft** *which concerns our physical necessities*
[158] **Reinigkeit = Reinheit**
[159] *blasphemy*
[160] *bountiful Lord!*

Geschlechte nicht weniger als bei dem Einzeln. Was erzogen wird, wird zu Etwas erzogen.

83

Die schmeichelnden Aussichten, die man dem Jünglinge eröffnet; die Ehre, der Wohlstand, die man ihm vorspiegelt: was sind sie mehr, als Mittel, ihn zum Manne zu erziehen, der auch dann, wenn diese Aussichten der Ehre und des Wohlstandes wegfallen, seine Pflicht zu tun vermögend sei. 5

84

Darauf zwecke die menschliche Erziehung ab: und die göttliche reiche dahin nicht? [161] Was der Kunst mit dem Einzeln gelingt, sollte der Natur nicht auch mit dem Ganzen gelingen? Lästerung! Lästerung! 10

85

Nein; sie wird kommen, sie wird gewiß kommen, die Zeit der Vollendung, da der Mensch, je überzeugter sein Verstand einer immer bessern Zukunft sich fühlet, von dieser Zukunft gleichwohl Bewegungsgründe [162] zu seinen Handlungen zu erborgen, nicht nötig haben wird; da er das Gute tun wird, weil es das Gute ist, nicht weil willkürliche [163] Belohnungen darauf gesetzt sind, 15

[161] **Darauf . . . nicht?** *Do you mean to say that human education has that as its goal, and divine education does not extend that far?*
[162] *motivating reasons, motivation*
[163] *arbitrary*

die seinen flatterhaften[164] Blick ehedem bloß heften und stärken sollten, die innern bessern Belohnungen desselben zu erkennen.

86

Sie wird gewiß kommen, die Zeit eines *neuen ewigen*
5 *Evangeliums,* die uns selbst in den Elementarbüchern des Neuen Bundes versprochen wird.

87

Vielleicht, daß selbst gewisse Schwärmer des dreizehnten und vierzehnten Jahrhunderts[165] einen Strahl dieses neuen ewigen Evangeliums aufgefangen hatten;
10 und nur darin irrten, daß sie den Ausbruch desselben so nahe verkündigten.

88

Vielleicht war ihr *dreifaches Alter der Welt* keine so leere Grille;[166] und gewiß hatten sie keine schlimme Absichten, wenn sie lehrten, daß der Neue Bund eben-
15 sowohl *antiquieret*[167] werden müsse, als es der Alte

[164] *wavering*
[165] Lessing is alluding to the concept of the three stages in the development of man that was preached by the abbot, Jacob of Floris (died A.D. 1202). The first stage was the "period of the father," which is represented by the Old Testament. The second stage, or "period of the son," came with the New Testament. The third stage, or "das ewige Evangelium," was to be brought by the "period of the Holy Ghost."
[166] *whim*
[167] *obsolete*

geworden. Es blieb auch bei ihnen immer die nämliche Ökonomie des nämlichen Gottes. Immer—sie meine Sprache sprechen zu lassen—der nämliche Plan der allgemeinen Erziehung des Menschengeschlechts.

89

Nur daß sie ihn übereilten; nur daß sie ihre Zeitgenossen, die noch kaum der Kindheit entwachsen waren, ohne Aufklärung, ohne Vorbereitung, mit eins zu Männern machen zu können glaubten, die ihres *dritten Zeitalters* würdig wären.

90

Und ebendas machte sie zu Schwärmern. Der Schwärmer tut oft sehr richtige Blicke in die Zukunft: aber er kann diese Zukunft nur nicht erwarten. Er wünscht diese Zukunft beschleuniget; und wünscht, daß sie durch ihn beschleuniget werde. Wozu sich die Natur Jahrtausende Zeit nimmt, soll in dem Augenblicke seines Daseins reifen. Denn was hat er davon, wenn das, was er für das Bessere erkennt, nicht noch bei seinen Lebzeiten das Bessere wird? Kömmt er wieder? Glaubt er wiederzukommen? —Sonderbar, daß diese Schwärmerei allein unter den Schwärmern nicht mehr Mode werden will!

91

Geh deinen unmerklichen Schritt, ewige Vorsehung! Nur laß mich dieser Unmerklichkeit wegen an dir nicht verzweifeln. —Laß mich an dir nicht verzweifeln, wenn selbst deine Schritte mir scheinen sollten, zurückzugehen!—Es ist nicht wahr, daß die kürzeste Linie immer die gerade ist.

92

5 Du hast auf deinem ewigen Wege so viel mitzunehmen! so viel Seitenschritte zu tun! —Und wie? wenn es nun gar so gut als ausgemacht wäre, daß das große langsame Rad, welches das Geschlecht seiner Vollkommenheit näher bringt, nur durch kleinere schnellere 10 Räder in Bewegung gesetzt würde, deren jedes sein Einzelnes ebendahin liefert?

93

Nicht anders! Eben die Bahn, auf welcher das Geschlecht zu seiner Vollkommenheit gelangt, muß jeder einzelne Mensch (der früher, der später) erst durch-15 laufen haben. —„In einem und eben demselben Leben durchlaufen haben? *Kann* er in eben demselben Leben ein sinnlicher Jude und ein geistiger Christ gewesen sein? Kann er in eben demselben Leben beide überholet haben?“

94

20 Das wohl nun nicht! —Aber warum könnte jeder einzelne Mensch auch nicht mehr als einmal auf dieser Welt vorhanden gewesen sein?

95

Ist diese Hypothese darum so lächerlich, weil sie die älteste ist? weil der menschliche Verstand, ehe ihn die Sophisterei der Schule zerstreut und geschwächt hatte, sogleich darauf verfiel?

96

Warum könnte auch ich nicht hier bereits einmal alle die Schritte zu meiner Vervollkommnung getan haben, welche bloß zeitliche Strafen und Belohnungen den Menschen bringen können?

97

Und warum nicht ein andermal alle die, welche zu tun, uns die Aussichten in ewige Belohnungen so mächtig helfen?

98

Warum sollte ich nicht so oft wiederkommen, als ich neue Kenntnisse, neue Fertigkeiten zu erlangen geschickt bin? Bringe ich auf einmal so viel weg, daß es der Mühe wiederzukommen etwa nicht lohnet?

99

Darum nicht? —Oder, weil ich es vergesse, daß ich schon dagewesen? Wohl mir, daß ich das vergesse. Die

Erinnerung meiner vorigen Zustände würde mir nur einen schlechten Gebrauch des gegenwärtigen zu machen erlauben. Und was ich auf itzt vergessen *muß*, habe ich denn das auf ewig vergessen?

100

5 Oder, weil so zuviel Zeit für mich verloren gehen würde? —Verloren? —Und was habe ich denn zu versäumen? Ist nicht die ganze Ewigkeit mein?

IMMANUEL KANT

[1724-1804]

BEANTWORTUNG DER FRAGE: WAS IST AUFKLÄRUNG?

IMMANUEL KANT is considered by many to be the greatest philosopher of modern times. He was born on April 22, 1824, in Königsberg, Prussia, and although his fame was spread throughout the learned world, he never traveled more than forty miles beyond the outskirts of his native city. His father had been a poor saddler, and poverty interfered with Kant's ambitions to finish his studies at the University of Königsberg. He was forced to spend the years 1746–1755 as a private tutor in order to accumulate enough money to finish his doctorate. After completing the doctorate in 1755, he became a lecturer at the university of his native city. His lectures encompassed logic, physics, mathematics, metaphysics, politics, physical geography, anthropology, natural theology, and pedagogy. In 1770 he finally received a promotion to professor, and he held "the chair of logic and metaphysics" until 1797.

Although Kant was slight in stature and physically

deformed, his well-regulated and disciplined personal life enabled him to accomplish enormous amounts of work. He was a prolific writer, and his long life enabled him to fill many volumes.

Kant's greatest contributions to philosophy are contained in his three great Critiques: *Kritik der reinen Vernunft* (1781); *Kritik der praktischen Vernunft* (1788); *Kritik der Urteilskraft* (1790). In the first of these famous Critiques Kant analyzes the limits of man's reason as an effective means of discovering truth. According to Kantian epistemology, real knowledge is limited to the perceptions of the senses, to experience. But the subject which perceives any given thing can never know the "thing in itself." He will always perceive the object in relation to his own faculties, which add to the object certain preconceived notions. Thus only the world of phenomena can be known to man. The world of the noumena, which lies beyond human experience, cannot be known rationally.

By placing limits on the cognitive ability of human reason, Kant went beyond his own era and opened up the way to the subjective philosophy of Schopenhauer and ultimately to the psychology of Freud.

In his second Critique, a discourse on ethics, Kant emphasizes the concept of duty. Man must act in accord with what is right and not according to his own likes and dislikes. This is essentially the meaning of his famous "categorical imperative." Kant's last Critique is in the area of aesthetics.

In 1794 Kant was reprimanded by royal decree for "Entstellung und Herabwürdigung mancher Haupt- und Grundlehren der Heiligen Schrift und des Christentums." He died in 1804, seven years after relinquishing his academic chair.

The intellectual of the eighteenth century was well aware of the fact that he was living in an era which had often been referred to as the Age of Enlightenment. But it was impossible to say exactly what this term signified. It is always extremely difficult for men to understand the implications of events which occur during their lifetime and in which they may be taking part. Many voices had asked the question: What is Enlightenment? In the following essay, which appeared in the *Berlinische Monatsschrift* (December 1784), Kant attempted to give an answer.

Bibliography

CASSIRER, ERNST, *Kants Leben und Lehre,* XI, *Immanuel Kants Werke,* edited by Ernst Cassirer. Berlin, 1912 ff.

DURANT, WILL, *The Story of Philosophy.* New York, 1926.

WALLACE, W., *Kant.* Oxford & London, 1882.

BEANTWORTUNG DER FRAGE: WAS IST AUFKLÄRUNG?

Aufklärung ist der Ausgang des Menschen aus seiner selbst verschuldeten Unmündigkeit.[1] *Unmündigkeit* ist das Unvermögen, sich [2] seines Verstandes ohne Leitung eines anderen zu bedienen.[2] *Selbstverschuldet* 5 ist diese Unmündigkeit, wenn die Ursache derselben [3] nicht am Mangel des Verstandes sondern der Entschließung und des Mutes [4] liegt, sich seiner [5] ohne Leitung eines andern zu bedienen. *Sapere aude!* [6] Habe Mut, dich deines *eigenen* Verstandes zu bedienen! ist 10 also der Wahlspruch der Aufklärung.

Faulheit und Feigheit sind die Ursachen, warum ein so großer Teil der Menschen, nachdem sie die Natur [7] längst von fremder Leitung frei gesprochen (*naturaliter majorennes*),[8] dennoch gerne zeitlebens unmündig 15 bleiben; und warum es anderen so leicht wird, sich zu deren Vormündern aufzuwerfen.[9] Es ist so bequem, unmündig zu sein. Habe ich ein Buch, das für mich

[1] **aus seiner selbst verschuldeten Unmündigkeit** *from his self-imposed immaturity.*

[2] **sich . . . zu bedienen** *to make use of, to avail oneself of*

[3] **derselben** *of it*

[4] **sondern [am Mangel] der Entschließung und des Mutes**

[5] **seiner** *of it,* i.e., **des Verstandes**

[6] **sapere aude** *dare to know*

[7] **die Natur** is the subject of the clause.

[8] **naturaliter majorennes** *naturally mature*

[9] **sich zu deren Vormündern aufzuwerfen** *to set themselves up as their guardians.*

Verstand hat,[10] einen Seelsorger,[11] der für mich Gewissen hat, einen Arzt, der für mich die Diät beurteilt usw., so brauche ich mich ja nicht selbst zu bemühen. Ich habe nicht nötig zu denken, wenn ich nur bezahlen kann; andere werden das verdrießliche Geschäft schon [12] für mich übernehmen. Daß der bei weitem größte Teil der Menschen (darunter das ganze schöne Geschlecht) den Schritt zur Mündigkeit, außer dem daß er beschwerlich ist, auch für sehr gefährlich halte, dafür sorgen schon jene Vormünder, die die Oberaufsicht über sie gütigst auf sich genommen haben.[13] Nachdem sie ihr Hausvieh zuerst dumm gemacht haben und sorgfältig verhüteten, daß diese ruhigen Geschöpfe ja keinen Schritt außer dem Gängelwagen,[14] darin sie sie einsperreten, wagen durften, so zeigen sie ihnen nachher die Gefahr, die ihnen drohet, wenn sie es versuchen, allein zu gehen. Nun ist diese Gefahr zwar eben so groß nicht, denn sie würden durch einigemal Fallen wohl endlich gehen lernen; allein [15] ein Beispiel von der Art macht doch schüchtern und schreckt gemeiniglich [16] von allen ferneren Versuchen ab.

Es ist also für jeden einzelnen Menschen schwer, sich aus der ihm beinahe zur Natur gewordenen Unmündigkeit [17] herauszuarbeiten. Er hat sie sogar lieb-

[10] **Habe ich ein Buch, das für mich Verstand hat** *If I have a book that supplies me with understanding* (*i.e., so that I do not have to use my own*), *that does my thinking for me*

[11] **Seelsorger** *pastor*

[12] **schon** *surely*

[13] Construe: **Jene Vormünder sorgen schon dafür, daß der größte Teil der Menschen den Schritt zur Mündigkeit auch für sehr gefährlich halte . . .**

[14] **Gängelwagen** *gocart*

[15] **allein** *however*

[16] **gemeiniglich** (archaic) *generally*

[17] **der ihm beinahe zur Natur gewordenen Unmündigkeit** *immaturity which has become almost second nature to him*

gewonnen [18] und ist vorderhand [19] wirklich unfähig, sich seines eigenen Verstandes zu bedienen, weil man ihn niemals den Versuch davon machen ließ. Satzungen und Formeln, diese mechanischen Werkzeuge eines
5 vernünftigen Gebrauchs oder vielmehr Mißbrauchs seiner Naturgaben, sind die Fußschellen einer immerwährenden Unmündigkeit.[20] Wer sie auch abwürfe,[21] würde dennoch auch über den schmalesten Graben einen nur unsicheren Sprung tun, weil er zu der-
10 gleichen freier Bewegung nicht gewöhnt ist. Daher gibt es nur wenige, denen es gelungen ist, durch eigene Bearbeitung ihres Geistes sich aus der Unmündigkeit herauszuwickeln und dennoch einen sicheren Gang zu tun.[22]

15 Daß aber ein Publikum sich selbst aufkläre, ist eher möglich; ja es ist, wenn man ihm nur Freiheit läßt, beinahe unausbleiblich. Denn da werden sich immer einige Selbstdenkende, sogar unter den eingesetzten Vormündern des großen Haufens finden,[23] welche,
20 nachdem sie das Joch der Unmündigkeit selbst abgeworfen haben, den Geist einer vernünftigen Schätzung des eigenen Werts und des Berufs jedes Menschen, selbst zu denken, um sich verbreiten werden.[24] Besonders ist hiebei: daß das Publikum,
25 welches zuvor von ihnen unter dieses Joch gebracht worden, sie hernach selbst zwingt, darunter zu bleiben,

[18] **liebgewinnen** *to become fond of*

[19] **vorderhand** *for the present*

[20] **Satzungen und Formeln . . . Unmündigkeit** *Precepts and formulae, these mechanical tools of rational usage, or rather misusage of his natural talents, are the fetters of perpetual immaturity.*

[21] **Wer sie auch abwürfe** *Whoever might throw them off*

[22] **einen sicheren Gang zu tun** *to step firmly*

[23] **da werden sich . . . finden** *there will be*

[24] **den Geist . . . um sich verbreiten werden** *will spread about them the spirit of a sensible estimate of their own worth and of the job of every human being to think for himself.*

wenn es von einigen seiner Vormünder, die selbst aller Aufklärung unfähig sind, dazu aufgewiegelt worden;[25] so schädlich ist es, Vorurteile zu pflanzen, weil sie sich zuletzt an denen selbst[26] rächen, die oder deren Vorgänger ihre Urheber gewesen sind. Daher kann ein Publikum nur langsam zur Aufklärung gelangen. Durch eine Revolution wird vielleicht wohl ein Abfall von persönlichen Despotism[27] und gewinnsüchtiger oder herrschsüchtiger Bedrückung, aber niemals wahre Reform der Denkungsart zustande kommen;[28] sondern neue Vorurteile werden, ebensowohl als die alten, zum Leitbande des gedankenlosen großen Haufens dienen.

Zu dieser Aufklärung aber wird nichts erfordert als *Freiheit;* und zwar die unschädlichste unter allem, was nur Freiheit heißen mag, nämlich die: von seiner Vernunft in allen Stücken[29] *öffentlichen Gebrauch* zu machen. Nur höre ich aber von allen Seiten rufen: *räsoniert nicht!* Der Offizier sagt: Räsoniert nicht, sondern exerziert! Der Finanzrat: Räsoniert nicht, sondern bezahlt! Der Geistliche: Räsoniert nicht, sondern glaubt! (Nur ein einziger Herr[30] in der Welt sagt: *Räsoniert,* so viel ihr wollt und worüber ihr wollt, *aber gehorcht!*) Hier ist überall Einschränkung der Freiheit. Welche Einschränkung aber ist der Aufklärung hinderlich, welche nicht, sondern ihr wohl gar beförderlich?[31]

[25] daß . . . worden *that the public which had previously been brought under this yoke by them (the now enlightened guardians) will afterwards itself compel them (the guardians) to remain under it whenever it has been incited to this by some of its* [*other*] *guardians who are themselves incapable of any enlightenment.*

[26] an denen selbst *on the very ones*

[27] Despotism = Despotismus

[28] wird zustande kommen *will be brought about*

[29] in allen Stücken *in all respects*

[30] Friedrich der Große

[31] sondern ihr wohl gar beförderlich *but probably quite beneficial to it*

—Ich antworte: der *öffentliche* Gebrauch seiner Vernunft muß jederzeit frei sein, und der allein kann Aufklärung unter Menschen zustande bringen; der *Privatgebrauch* derselben aber darf öfters sehr enge eingeschränkt sein, ohne doch darum den Fortschritt der Aufklärung sonderlich zu hindern. Ich verstehe aber unter dem öffentlichen Gebrauche seiner eigenen Vernunft denjenigen, den jemand als *Gelehrter* von ihr vor dem ganzen Publikum der *Leserwelt* macht.[32] Den Privatgebrauch nenne ich denjenigen, den er in einem gewissen ihm anvertrauten *bürgerlichen Posten* oder Amte [33] von seiner Vernunft machen darf. Nun ist zu manchen Geschäften, die in das Interesse des gemeinen Wesens laufen, ein gewisser Mechanism notwendig, vermittelst dessen [34] einige Glieder des gemeinen Wesens [35] sich bloß passiv verhalten müssen, um durch eine künstliche [36] Einhelligkeit von der Regierung zu öffentlichen Zwecken [37] gerichtet oder wenigstens von der Zerstörung dieser Zwecke abgehalten zu werden.[38] Hier ist es nun freilich nicht erlaubt zu räsonnieren; sondern man muß gehorchen. Sofern sich [39] aber dieser Teil der Maschine zugleich als Glied eines ganzen gemeinen Wesens, ja sogar der Weltbürgergesellschaft ansieht,[39] mithin [40] in der Qualität [41] eines Gelehrten,

[32] **denjenigen . . . macht** *that which someone makes of it as a scholar before the entire reading public.*

[33] **in einem . . . Amte** *in a particular civil post or office that has been entrusted to him*

[34] **vermittelst dessen** *by means of which*

[35] **des gemeinen Wesens** *of the community*

[36] **künstlich** *artificial*

[37] **öffentlichen Zwecken** *public aims*

[38] **abgehalten zu werden** *to be restrained*

[39] **sich ansehen** *to regard oneself*

[40] **mithin** *thus*

[41] **in der Qualität** *in the capacity*

der sich an ein Publikum im eigentlichen Verstande [42] durch Schriften wendet, kann er allerdings räsonnieren, ohne daß dadurch die Geschäfte leiden, zu denen er zum Teile als passives Glied angesetzt ist. So würde es sehr verderblich sein, wenn ein Offizier, 5 dem von seinen Oberen etwas anbefohlen wird, im Dienste über die Zweckmäßigkeit oder Nützlichkeit dieses Befehls laut vernünfteln [43] wollte; er muß gehorchen. Es kann ihm aber billigermaßen [44] nicht verwehrt werden,[45] als Gelehrter über die Fehler im Kriegesdienste 10 Anmerkungen zu machen und diese seinem Publikum zur Beurteilung vorzulegen. Der Bürger kann sich nicht weigern, die ihm auferlegten Abgaben zu leisten; [46] sogar kann ein vorwitziger Tadel solcher Auflagen,[47] wenn sie von ihm geleistet werden sollen, 15 als ein Skandal, (das allgemeine Widersetzlichkeiten veranlassen könnte), bestraft werden. Ebenderselbe handelt demohngeachtet der Pflicht eines Bürgers nicht entgegen,[48] wenn er als Gelehrter wider die Unschicklichkeit oder auch Ungerechtigkeit solcher Aus- 20 schreibungen [49] öffentlich seine Gedanken äußert. Ebenso ist ein Geistlicher [50] verbunden, seinen Katechismusschülern und seiner Gemeine [51] nach dem Symbol [52] der Kirche, der er dient, seinen Vortrag zu tun,

[42] **im eigentlichen Verstande** *literally*
[43] **vernünfteln** *quibble*
[44] **billigermaßen** *in all fairness*
[45] **verwehrt werden** *be prevented from*
[46] **die ihm auferlegten Abgaben zu leisten** *to pay the taxes imposed upon him*
[47] **socher Auflagen** *of such levies*
[48] **Ebenderselbe . . . entgegen** *The very same person is nevertheless not acting contrary to his duty as a citizen*
[49] **solcher Ausschreibungen** *of such tax impositions*
[50] **Geistlicher** *clergyman*
[51] **Gemeine = Gemeinde** *parish*
[52] **nach dem Symbol** *according to the creed*

denn er ist auf diese Bedingung [53] angenommen worden. Aber als Gelehrter hat er volle Freiheit, ja sogar den Beruf dazu, alle seine sorgfältig geprüften und wohlmeinenden Gedanken über das Fehlerhafte
5 in jenem Symbol und Vorschläge wegen [54] besserer Einrichtung des Religions- und Kirchenwesens [55] dem Publikum mitzuteilen. Es ist hiebei auch nichts,[56] was dem Gewissen zur Last gelegt werden könnte. Denn was er zufolge seines Amts als Geschäftträger der
10 Kirche lehrt, das stellt er als etwas vor, in Ansehung dessen [57] er nicht freie Gewalt hat, nach eigenem Gutdünken [58] zu lehren, sondern das er nach Vorschrift und im Namen eines andern vorzutragen angestellt ist. Er wird sagen: unsere Kirche lehrt dieses oder jenes;
15 das sind die Beweisgründe, deren sie sich bedient. Er zieht alsdann allen praktischen Nutzen für seine Gemeinde aus Satzungen, die er selbst nicht mit voller Überzeugung unterschreiben würde,[59] zu deren Vortrag er sich gleichwohl anheischig machen kann,[60] weil es
20 doch nicht ganz unmöglich ist, daß darin Wahrheit verborgen läge, auf alle Fälle aber wenigstens doch nichts der innern Religion Widersprechendes darin angetroffen wird.[61] Denn glaubte er das letztere darin zu finden, so würde er sein Amt mit Gewissen [62] nicht

[53] **auf diese Bedingung** *on this condition*
[54] **wegen** *regarding*
[55] **Religions- und Kirchenwesens** *of religious and church affairs*
[56] **Es ist hiebei auch nichts** *There is also nothing in this*
[57] **in Ansehung dessen** *regarding which*
[58] **Gutdünken** *judgment, discretion*
[59] **nicht unterschreiben würden** *would not subscribe to*
[60] **zu deren . . . kann** *which he can nevertheless undertake to lecture upon*
[61] **auf alle Fälle . . . wird** *but in any case, at least nothing is encountered in it that contradicts inner religion* (*i.e., that goes against his inner convictions*)
[62] **mit Gewissen** *in good conscience*

verwalten können; er müßte es niederlegen. Der Gebrauch also, den ein angestellter Lehrer von seiner Vernunft vor seiner Gemeinde macht, ist bloß ein *Privatgebrauch,* weil diese immer nur eine häusliche,[63] obzwar noch so große Versammlung ist; und in Ansehung dessen [64] ist er als Priester nicht frei und darf es auch nicht sein, weil er einen fremden Auftrag ausrichtet. Dagegen als Gelehrter, der durch Schriften zum eigentlichen publikum, nämlich der Welt spricht, mithin [65] der Geistliche im *öffentlichen Gebrauche* seiner Vernunft, genießt einer uneingeschränkten Freiheit, sich seiner eigenen Vernunft zu bedienen und in seiner eigenen Person zu sprechen. Denn daß die Vormünder des Volks (in geistlichen Dingen) selbst wieder unmündig sein sollen, ist eine Ungereimtheit, die auf Verewigung der Ungereimtheiten hinausläuft.[66]

Aber sollte nicht eine Gesellschaft von Geistlichen, etwa eine Kirchenversammlung [67] oder eine ehrwürdige Classis [67] (wie sie sich unter den Holländern selbst nennt), berechtigt sein, sich eidlich auf ein gewisses unveränderliches Symbol zu verpflichten,[68] um so eine unaufhörliche Obervormundschaft [69] über jedes ihrer Glieder und vermittelst ihrer [70] über das Volk zu führen und diese so gar [71] zu verewigen? Ich sage: das ist ganz unmöglich. Ein solcher Kontrakt, der auf immer alle weitere Aufklärung vom Menschengeschlechte abzu-

[63] **häusliche** *domestic*
[64] **in Ansehung dessen** *in consideration of this*
[65] *thus*
[66] **hinauslaufen** *to amount to*
[67] **Kirchenversammlung, Classis** *synod*
[68] **sich eidlich verpflichten** *to commit oneself by oath*
[69] **Obervormundschaft** *senior guardianship*
[70] **ihrer** *of it*
[71] **so gar = sogar**

halten geschlossen würde,[72] ist schlechterdings null und nichtig; und sollte er auch [73] durch die oberste Gewalt, durch Reichstage und die feierlichsten Friedensschlüsse bestätigt sein. Ein Zeitalter kann sich nicht verbünden
5 und darauf verschwören, das folgende [74] in einen Zustand zu setzen, darin [75] es ihm unmöglich werden muß, seine (vornehmlich so sehr angelegentliche [76]) Erkenntnisse zu erweitern, von Irrtümern zu reinigen und überhaupt in der Aufklärung weiterzuschreiten.
10 Das wäre ein Verbrechen wider die menschliche Natur, deren ursprüngliche Bestimmung gerade in diesem Fortschreiten besteht; und die Nachkommen [77] sind also vollkommen dazu berechtigt, jene Beschlüsse, als unbefugter und frevelhafter Weise genommen,[78] zu ver-
15 werfen. Der Probierstein [79] alles dessen, was über ein Volk als Gesetz beschlossen werden kann, liegt in der Frage: ob ein Volk sich selbst wohl ein solches Gesetz auferlegen könnte? Nun wäre dieses wohl, gleichsam [80] in der Erwartung eines bessern, auf eine bestimmte
20 kurze Zeit möglich, um eine gewisse Ordnung einzuführen: indem man es zugleich jedem der Bürger, vornehmlich dem Geistlichen, frei ließe, in der Qualität eines Gelehrten [81] öffentlich, d. i. durch Schriften, über das Fehlerhafte der dermaligen Einrichtung [82] seine

[72] Construe: **der geschlossen würde, um alle weitere Aufklärung vom Menschengeschlechte auf immer abzuhalten.**

[73] **und sollte er auch** *and even if it should*

[74] **das folgende [Zeitalter]**

[75] **darin = worin**

[76] **vornehmlich so sehr angelegentliche** *chiefly so very urgent*

[77] **Nachkommen** *descendants, posterity*

[78] **als unbefugter . . . genommen** *as having been made without authority and outrageously*

[79] **Probierstein** *touchstone*

[80] **gleichsam** *as it were*

[81] **in der Qualität eines Gelehrten** *in the capacity of a scholar*

[82] **das Fehlerhafte der dermaligen Einrichtung** *the deficiency of the institution of that time*

Anmerkungen zu machen, indessen [83] die eingeführte Ordnung noch immer fortdauerte, bis die Einsicht [84] in die Beschaffenheit dieser Sachen öffentlich so weit gekommen und bewähret worden,[85] daß sie durch Vereinigung ihrer Stimmen (wenngleich nicht aller) einen Vorschlag vor den Thron bringen könnte, um diejenigen Gemeinden in Schutz zu nehmen, die sich etwa nach ihren Begriffen der besseren Einsicht zu einer veränderten Religionseinrichtung geeinigt hätten, ohne doch diejenigen zu hindern, die es beim alten wollten bewenden lassen.[86] Aber auf eine beharrliche, von niemanden [sic] öffentlich zu bezweifelnde Religionsverfassung [87] auch nur binnen der Lebensdauer eines Menschen sich zu einigen, und dadurch einen Zeitraum in dem Fortgange der Menschheit zur Verbesserung gleichsam zu vernichten und fruchtlos,[88] dadurch aber wohl gar der Nachkommenschaft nachteilig [89] zu machen, ist schlechterdings unerlaubt. Ein Mensch kann zwar für seine Person und auch alsdann nur auf einige Zeit in dem, was ihm zu wissen obliegt,[90] die Aufklärung aufschieben; aber auf sie Verzicht zu tun,[91] es sei für seine Person, mehr aber noch für die Nachkommenschaft,[92] heißt die heiligen Rechte der Menschheit verletzen und mit Füßen treten. Was aber nicht einmal ein Volk über sich selbst beschließen darf,

[83] **indessen** *while*
[84] **Einsicht** *insight, understanding*
[85] **bewähret worden** *been established as true*
[86] **die es beim alten wollten bewenden lassen** *who wanted to rest satisfied with the old*
[87] **Religionsverfassung** *religious system*
[88] **fruchtlos [zu machen]**
[89] *detrimental*
[90] **was ihm zu wissen obliegt** *what it is necessary for him to know*
[91] **aber auf sie Verzicht zu tun** *but to renounce it*
[92] **es sei . . . die Nachkommenschaft** *for himself and even more so for posterity*

das darf noch weniger ein Monarch über das Volk beschließen; denn sein gesetzgebendes Ansehen beruht eben darauf, daß er den gesamten Volkswillen in dem seinigen vereinigt. Wenn er nur darauf sieht,[93] daß alle
5 wahre oder vermeinte Verbesserung mit der bürgerlichen Ordnung zusammenbestehe,[94] so kann er seine Untertanen übrigens nur selbst machen lassen, was sie um ihres Seelenheils willen [95] zu tun nötig finden; das geht ihn nichts an,[96] wohl aber zu verhüten,[97] daß nicht
10 einer den andern gewalttätig hindere, an der Bestimmung und Beförderung desselben nach allem seinen Vermögen zu arbeiten. Es tut selbst seiner Majestät Abbruch,[98] wenn er sich hierin mischt, indem er die Schriften, wodurch seine Untertanen ihre Einsichten
15 ins reine zu bringen [99] suchen, seiner Regierungsaufsicht würdigt, sowohl wenn er dieses aus eigener höchsten Einsicht tut, wo er sich dem Vorwurfe aussetzt: *Caesar non est supra grammaticos,*[100] als auch und noch weit mehr, wenn er seine oberste Gewalt soweit
20 erniedrigt, den geistlichen Despotism einiger Tyrannen in seinem Staate gegen seine übrigen Untertanen zu unterstützen.

Wenn denn nun gefragt wird: leben wir jetzt in einem *aufgeklärten* Zeitalter? so ist die Antwort: Nein,
25 aber wohl in einem Zeitalter der *Aufklärung.* Daß die Menschen, wie die Sachen jetzt stehen, im ganzen

[93] **Wenn er nur darauf sieht** *If he only sees to it*
[94] **mit der bürgerlichen Ordnung zusammenbestehe** *is compatible with the civil order*
[95] **um ihres Seelenheils willen** *for the good of their souls*
[96] **das geht ihn nichts an** *that is not his concern*
[97] **wohl aber zu verhüten** *but it certainly is [his concern] to guard against*
[98] **Abbruch tun** *be harmful to, injure*
[99] **ins reine zu bringen** *to clarify*
[100] *Caesar is not above grammarians*

genommen,[101] schon imstande wären oder darin auch nur gesetzt werden könnten, in Religionsdingen sich ihres eigenen Verstandes ohne Leitung eines andern sicher und gut zu bedienen, daran fehlt noch sehr viel. Allein, daß jetzt ihnen doch das Feld geöffnet wird, sich dahin frei zu bearbeiten und die Hindernisse der allgemeinen Aufklärung oder des Ausganges aus ihrer selbstverschuldeten Unmündigkeit allmählich weniger werden, davon haben wir doch deutliche Anzeigen. In diesem Betracht ist dieses Zeitalter das Zeitalter der Aufklärung oder das Jahrhundert FRIEDERICHS.[102]

Ein Fürst, der es seiner nicht unwürdig findet [103] zu sagen, daß er es für *Pflicht* halte, in Religionsdingen den Menschen nichts vorzuschreiben, sondern ihnen darin volle Freiheit zu lassen, der also selbst den hochmütigen Namen der *Toleranz* von sich ablehnt,[104] ist selbst aufgeklärt und verdient von der dankbaren Welt und Nachwelt als derjenige gepriesen zu werden, der zuerst das menschliche Geschlecht der Unmündigkeit, wenigstens von seiten der Regierung, entschlug [105] und jedem frei ließ, sich in allem, was Gewissensangelegenheit ist, seiner eigenen Vernunft zu bedienen. Unter ihm dürfen verehrungswürdige Geistliche, unbeschadet ihrer Amtspflicht,[106] ihre vom angenommenen Symbol hier oder da abweichenden Urteile [107] und Einsichten

[101] **im ganzen genommen** *all in all*
[102] **Friedrichs des Großen**
[103] **der es seiner nicht unwürdig findet** *who does not find it unworthy of himself*
[104] **von sich ablehnt** *refuses for himself*
[105] **entschlug** *divested*
[106] **unbeschadet ihrer Amtspflicht** *without prejudice to their official duty*
[107] **ihre vom angenommenen . . . Urteile** *their judgments which* deviate here or there from the accepted creed

in der Qualität der Gelehrten frei und öffentlich der Welt zur Prüfung darlegen; noch mehr aber jeder andere, der durch keine Amtspflicht eingeschränkt ist. Dieser Geist der Freiheit breitet sich auch außerhalb 5 aus, selbst da, wo er mit äußeren Hindernissen einer sich selbst mißverstehenden Regierung[108] zu ringen hat. Denn es leuchtet dieser doch ein Beispiel vor, daß bei Freiheit für die öffentliche Ruhe und Einigkeit des gemeinen Wesens nicht das mindeste zu besorgen 10 sei. Die Menschen arbeiten sich von selbst nach und nach aus der Rohigkeit[109] heraus, wenn man nur nicht absichtlich künstelt,[110] um sie darin zu erhalten.

Ich habe den Hauptpunkt der Aufklärung, d. i. des 15 Ausganges der Menschen aus ihrer selbstverschuldeten Unmündigkeit, vorzüglich in *Religionssachen* gesetzt, weil in Ansehung der Künste und Wissenschaften unsere Beherrscher kein Interesse haben, den Vormund über ihre Untertanen zu spielen, überdem auch jene 20 Unmündigkeit, so wie die schädlichste, also auch die entehrendste unter allen ist. Aber die Denkungsart eines Staatsoberhaupts, der die erstere begünstigt, geht noch weiter und sieht ein: daß selbst in Ansehung seiner *Gesetzgebung* es ohne Gefahr sei, seinen Unter-25 tanen zu erlauben, von ihrer eigenen Vernunft *öffentlichen* Gebrauch zu machen und ihre Gedanken über eine bessere Abfassung derselben, sogar mit einer freimütigen Kritik der schon gegebenen,[111] der Welt öffent-

[108] **einer sich selbst mißverstehenden Regierung** *of a government which does not understand itself* (*i.e., which attempts to rule in matters which should not concern it*)
[109] **Rohigkeit = Roheit**
[110] **künstelt** *takes pains*
[111] **der schon gegebenen [Gesetzgebung]**

lich vorzulegen; davon [112] wir ein glänzendes Beispiel haben, wodurch noch kein Monarch demjenigen vorging, welchen wir verehren.

Aber auch nur derjenige, der, selbst aufgeklärt, sich nicht vor Schatten fürchtet, zugleich aber ein wohl- 5 disziplinertes zahlreiches Heer zum Bürgen [113] der öffentlichen Ruhe zur Hand [114] hat,— kann das sagen, was ein Freistaat nicht wagen darf. *Räsoniert, soviel ihr wollt, und worüber ihr wollt; nur gehorcht!* So zeigt sich hier ein befremdlicher, nicht erwarteter Gang [115] 10 menschlicher Dinge; sowie auch sonst, wenn man ihn im großen betrachtet, darin fast alles paradox ist. Ein größerer Grad bürgerlicher Freiheit scheint der Freiheit des *Geistes* des Volks vorteilhaft und setzt ihr doch unübersteigliche Schranken; ein Grad weniger von 15 jener [116] verschafft hingegen diesem Raum,[117] sich nach allem seinen Vermögen auszubreiten. Wenn denn die Natur unter dieser harten Hülle den Keim, für den sie am zärtlichsten sorgt, nämlich den Hang und Beruf zum *freien Denken*, ausgewickelt hat: so wirkt dieser 20 allmählich zurück auf die Sinnesart [118] des Volks, (wodurch dies der *Freiheit zu handeln* nach und nach fähiger wird), und endlich auch sogar auf die Grundsätze der *Regierung*, die es ihr selbst zuträglich findet,[119]

[112] **davon = wovon**
[113] **zum Bürgen** *for the safety, to insure*
[114] **zur Hand** *at his disposal*
[115] **ein befremdlicher, nicht erwarteter Gang** *a surprising, unexpected course*
[116] **von jener [Freiheit]**
[117] **verschafft hingegen diesem Raum** *on the other hand provides the latter* (**i.e., dem Volk**) *with space*
[118] **Sinnesart** *character*
[119] **die es ihr selbst zuträglich findet** *which finds it profitable for itself*

den Menschen, der nun *mehr als Maschine* ist, seiner Würde gemäß zu behandeln.*

Königsberg in Preußen, den 30. Septemb. 1784

I. Kant

* In den *Büsching*schen Wöchentlichen Nachrichten vom 13. Sept. lese ich heute den 30. ebendess.[120] die Anzeige der Berlinischen Monatsschrift von diesem Monat, worin des Herrn *Mendelssohn*[121] Beantwortung ebenderselben Frage angeführt wird. Mir ist sie noch nicht zu Händen gekommen; sonst würde sie die gegenwärtige zurückgehalten haben, die jetzt nur zum Versuche dastehen mag, wiefern der Zufall Einstimmigkeit der Gedanken zuwege bringen könne.

[120] **ebendess = ebendesselben Monats**

[121] **Moses Mendelssohn** (1729–1786), a friend of Lessing who is best known for his treatise on the immortality of the soul, *Phädon, oder über die Unsterblichkeit der Seele* (1767).